WELL FED

PALEO RECIPES FOR PEOPLE WHO LOVE TO EAT

BY MELISSA JOULWAN
Foreword by Melissa and Dallas Hartwig
Photos by David Humphreys
Design by Kathleen Shannon

WELL FED: PALEO RECIPES FOR PEOPLE WHO LOVE TO EAT

WELL FED: PALEO RECIPES FOR PEOPLE WHO LOVE TO EAT

Author: Melissa Joulwan
Foreword: Melissa and Dallas Hartwig
Copy Editor: Alison Finney
Assistant Copy Editor: Walker Fenz
Photography: David Humphreys
Illustrations: David Humphreys
Design: Kathleen Shannon

ISBN 10: 0-615-57226-X
ISBN 13: 978-0-615-57226-0

Published by:
Smudge Publishing, LLC
344 Fairview Terrace
White River Junction, VT 05001
www.smudgepublishing.com

11th printing, March 2015

smudge
PUBLISHING

TO THE ENTIRE JOULWAN AND STRAMARA CLANS — AND THE SPIRIT
OF MY SITTI — FOR ALL THE FOOD AND LOVE, AND FOOD-LOVE

AND TO MY HUSBAND DAVE, WHO IS MY FAVORITE DINNER COMPANION

THANK YOU

To Bethany Benzur, for bringing us together with Kathleen Shannon

To Nathan Black, for taking the *Well Fed* team photos and making us all look so good

To Tannen Campbell, Cameron Siewert, and Blake Howard, for the generous contribution of their big brains and senses of humor to the book title brainstorm (and an additional hug of appreciation to Tannen for her one-of-a-kind bowls)

To Stefanie DiStefano, for her made-with-love pottery and magical energy

To Stacey Doyle, for being a voluntary recipe tester and playing "You Know How You Could Do That?" during our work lunches

To Walker Fenz, for detail-obsessed editing and proofing

To Alison Finney, for approaching her sharp-eyed copy editing with eagerness, then delivering her recommendations with a gentle touch

To Melissa and Dallas Hartwig, for showing us the way to love food again and for applying their giant brains to the cookbook manuscript

To Gray Luckett and Chris Lynn, for living without some of their bowls, plates, and cutlery for a few months so we had props for photos

To Cheryl McKay, for inspiring me with wild-caught salmon and for volunteering her legal eagle eyes at the eleventh hour

To Kathleen Shannon, for designing a cookbook that's both a how-to guide and a love letter to cooking real food

And to all the readers of my blog The Clothes Make The Girl, for testing my recipes, asking questions, and sharing their enthusiasm for this project when I needed it most

FOREWORD

"YOU DON'T HAVE TO COOK FANCY OR COMPLICATED MASTERPIECES — JUST GOOD FOOD FROM FRESH INGREDIENTS."

- Julia Child

We have a confession: Overall, we give our collective cooking skills a "B" grade at best. (Truthfully, one of us is pulling that average down, but we're not saying which one.) We're darn good nutritionists, but our background isn't in the culinary arts. The good news? We don't have to be Cordon Bleu-trained chefs, because we've got a well fed, dressed to kill, glossy haired, rock and roll, tart tongued secret weapon: our friend Mel.

First, she is a naturally gifted chef – but not the snooty kind who makes dishes better suited for an art gallery than a normal person's kitchen. No, she's the kind of chef who makes real food for real people, using simple, fresh ingredients designed to make you healthier. She's the kind of chef you'd want as your best friend or your next-door neighbor, both for her style and for her food. And her star has never shined more brightly than within the pages of this cookbook.

Flip through *Well Fed*, and you'll immediately see this isn't some taking-itself-so-seriously cookbook full of pictures you'd barely recognize as food. Mel created these recipes in her kitchen, using the same basic tools and equipment you've got in your kitchen. And she developed and prepared these meals around her own busy schedule – in between work, exercise, family, friends, and looking after a house and a husband and a cat. (The lesson: if she's got time to create them from scratch, you've got time to make them for dinner.) Because she knows that cooking is scary for lots of folks, she's filled her recipes with extra details, helpful hints, and technique tips. (No Ph.D. required!)

In addition, *Well Fed* meals don't demand fancy pants ingredients – it's all stuff you can pick up at your average grocery store or health food market. (Don't be intimidated by the spices, just polish your measuring spoons and dive on in.) Finally, Mel understands that treats and sweets are a normal part of most peoples' sustainable diet, but we don't need yet another "healthy" brownie recipe. We need inspiration to make our *everyday* food new, fresh, and exciting. That's why almost all of the *Well Fed* recipes are Whole30 approved, perfect for both our nutrition program and your everyday meals. (And when you decide to kick up your heels, there's one sinful-looking dessert on page 151 that should hit the spot, but won't make you feel like you swallowed a brick.)

The best part about *Well Fed*? Mel stamps her irreverent brand onto every dish, combining simple, fresh ingredients in ways you'd never expect. It's healthy eating like you've never seen it – a collision of flavors, textures, and colors designed to impress your eyes, stimulate your taste buds, and nourish your body.

We believe the purpose of a cookbook is not to cook for you or even to teach you how to cook. Instead, the right cookbook will inspire you to discover your own creativity and tastes, and establish your own experiences and traditions. *Well Fed* was written to do just that, and will effortlessly allow you to cultivate your own rock star inner chef.

Bon appétit!

Best,
Dallas & Melissa Hartwig
Founders, Whole9
Creators of the Whole30 program

TABLE OF CONTENTS

First Week's Winners
Share Their Recipes

ompletely
ut equally
pes for soups
re selected by
Your-Recipe"
winners for the
f the seventh
t sponsored by
CAN.

s, all of whom
icipated in
ests were Mrs.
Joulwan of
or her Italian
Cioppina," Mrs.
Grickis of
ille for her
wder" and Mrs.
sh of Schuylkill
er "Dilled Lamb

lwan, whose
homas Joulwan
the Country
aurant, has a
rest in recipes
r association in
ness. She chose
ing one, a
of fish, seafood
complements,
collection of
and clippings
sections of
This is her first
in the weekly
hough last year
an Honorable
t to become a
in the final
the Necho Allen
stand-in for one
nners who could
and earned top

preparation of a baby food
to her menus in October,
when she expects to
increase her family. Her out-
of-the-kitchen activities
include membership in
the Orwigsburg Woman's
League.

Mrs. Grickis has an
unbroken record for six
years as a top winner in the
weekly contest. This year
her husband Timothy's
enthusiasm for the
"Cheesey Chowder" was the
reason for its selection as
her entry. His choise was
apparently that of the
judges for it kept her
winning streak going. Mrs.
Grickis, who prefers
simplicity in a good recipe,
added the cheese to a basic
recipe she got from her
mother, because her family
likes cheese and the
chowder is hearty enough
for a complete meal. The
family for which Mrs.
Grickis makes a hobby of
cooking, is comprised of
three children, Timmy, Jr.,
aged seven, Tracy Jane, two
years old, and Tarajane,
eight months. A den mother
for the Cub Scouts, an
assistant Brownie leader, an
officer in the Catholic
Daughters, and a member of
the Port Carbon St.
Stephen's Church School
Mothers Club, the winner
still finds time for her first
love, cooking.

try, with her recipe for
"Tomato Aspic Salad",
merited an Honorable
Mention for her "Raspberry
Parfait," and then won
second place in the Cook-Off
at the culmination of the
contest.

Mrs. Windish, the
grandmother of six, has one
son Charles, living in Akron,
Ohio. She is a widow who
keeps interested in many
things, including helping
other people, doing things
for her church, (Christ
Lutheran in Schuylkill
Haven) and keeping up with
sports events. For
relaxation, she crochets,
and has completed a number
of afghans and doilies.

Her winning recipes have
come from a combination of
recipes she has seen in
cookbooks, and then using
her own knowledge of food
combinations, has added
some of her favorite
ingredients to come up with
a "Special" dish that is all
her own, until she shares it
with the readers of the
REPUBLICAN in the recipe
contest.

The food-knowledgeable
judges had a difficult task in
selecting the ten Honorable
Mention winners from the
first week's tremendous
response to the Soups and
Stews category. There were
11 of equal merit in their
opinions, and rather than
eliminate one to keep the

MRS. VERONICA JOULWAN
Orwigsburg

Cioppina

(Italian Fish Stew)

Serves 8

INGREDIENTS

2 lbs. haddock or halibut fillets
8 oz. canned, fresh, or frozen shrimp
½ cup chopped green pepper
¼ cup minced onion
2 cloves garlic, minced
¼ cup olive oil or salad oil
1 — 28 oz. can tomatoes, cut up

WELCOME TO WELL FED

I was born into a restaurant family.

Before you get the wrong idea, you should know a few facts: We lived in rural Pennsylvania, it was the late sixties, and no one was yet treating chefs like rock stars.

My grandfather owned The Garfield, one of those shiny chrome diners, where you could sit at the counter, sip on a bottomless cup of coffee, and wisecrack with the waitresses and other regulars. My dad ran The Country Squire Restaurant, a combination coffee shop, formal dining room, and motel.

I grew up in these restaurants and took my place in an extended family of cooks.

My dad at his first cooking job in the Poconos.

As a teen and young adult, I ate for pleasure, without too much concern for nutrition. Soon, even though I loved to eat and food was a major binding agent in my family, food became the enemy. I grew fat and unhealthy because I knew food, but I didn't know how to eat.

Now, because I follow a paleo diet, cooking and eating have again become a source of joy. Visualizing the meal, buying the healthy ingredients, chopping and stirring and working the alchemy that transforms ingredients into love in the form of food – these are a few of my favorite things.

My goal with this book is to teach you what I know about how to run a paleo kitchen and how to combine ingredients to become something truly nourishing for your body and soul and for the important people in your life.

The two essential tricks for happy, healthy eating are being prepared and avoiding boredom. *Well Fed* explains how to enjoy a "cookup" once a week so that you have ready-to-go food for snacks and meals every day. It will also show you how to mix and match basic ingredients with spices and seasonings that take your taste buds on a world tour.

I've kept the recipes as simple as possible, without compromising taste, and I've tested the recipes extensively to minimize work and maximize flavor. Where it makes sense, I've explained how you can cut corners on technique and when you'll have the best results if you follow my instructions. Some of the dishes are "project recipes," so I've included prep and cooking time to indicate which are quick enough for weeknights and which are perfect for lazy Sunday afternoons.

I'm from a melting pot family: Lebanese on Dad's side, Italian and Slovak on Mom's. From the time I could shove food into my mouth, I ate kibbeh and eggplant parmesan, and while Mom taught me to cook pancakes on weekend mornings, I picked up my dad's tricks for making baba ghanoush at dinner. The recipes in this book reflect my affection for traditional ethnic cuisines and for foods with contrasting flavors and textures, so that your healthy food also includes the luscious contrasts of sweet savory and crispy chewy.

Ultimately, I hope this book will make you feel that paleo eating – too often defined by what we give up – is really about what we gain: health, vitality, a light heart, and memorable meals to be shared with the people we love.

WHAT IS PALEO? WE CALL IT DINO-CHOW

You've probably heard the paleo diet called a lot of things. Caveman Diet. Primal. Real Food. Paleo Lifestyle. Around our house we call it "Dino-Chow." All of these terms refer to roughly the same way of eating that's based on the idea that we feel our best – and are our healthiest, mentally and physically – when we mimic the nutrition of our hunter-gatherer ancestors.

I know it sounds a little groovy or like something from science fiction. But evolutionary biologists, chemists, and nutritionists are really onto something. When we remove inflammatory foods from our diets – foods that were not part of our ancestors' daily meals – we reduce our risk for "diseases of civilization" like heart disease, diabetes, and cancers. Additionally, our energy levels are better, we look years younger, and we enjoy life more.

I know there were no dinosaurs in the Paleolithic Era, but dino-chow is a funny name, so just roll with the joke, please.

PALEO EXPERTS

To understand all of the science behind these nutritional guidelines, I recommend you turn to the same experts that educated me:

Whole9: Melissa and Dallas Hartwig are the big brains behind the wonderful Whole30 program that's helped thousands of people slay their sugar demons and create a new, healthy relationship with real food. They consume and digest all the paleo research so that foodies like us can simply learn how to eat. Thanks to Melissa and Dallas, I can now enjoy my food without measuring every meal or recording every bite in a food journal.

Robb Wolf: The author of *The Paleo Solution* goes deep into the geeky science with a sense of humor that makes it all easily understood and relevant to daily life. Robb's book broadened my understanding of the "why" behind the paleo lifestyle so it's easier to do the right "what" on a daily basis.

Mark Sisson: The author of *The Primal Blueprint* presents a compelling case for living more primally in every aspect of life: nutrition, exercise, sleep, socializing, and sex! I love what Mark has to say about finding time to play and taking advantage of modern conveniences without feeling beholden to a thoroughly modern (unhealthy) lifestyle.

Nora Gedgaudas: The author of *Primal Body, Primal Mind* explains how blood sugar swings – from too many carbohydrates, and inadequate protein and fat – contribute to mental illness and general unhappiness.

The Resources section (p. 156) includes more details about these mentors, as well as a comprehensive list of the sources I turn to for inspiration and information.

Let's get the bad news out of the way immediately: Paleo eating means avoiding many foods that top your list of favorites. Different paleo practitioners promote differing guidelines. I follow the standards outlined by Melissa and Dallas Hartwig of Whole9. The guidelines are fairly stringent, but they're based on the compelling idea that we should eat the foods that make us healthiest, and I can't argue with that.

My "No" List includes the following, and you won't find any of these foods in *Well Fed* recipes.

PROCESSED FOODS: As a former Doritos aficionado, I know it can be hard to give up junk food. But anything found in the middle of the grocery store, housed inside brightly-colored plastic or cardboard, is not a healthy choice.

GRAINS: Despite conventional wisdom, even whole grains are not a good idea. Grains include wheat, corn, oats, rice, quinoa, barley, and millet. They're to be avoided in all their devilish forms: bread, pasta, cereals, breading on fried foods, etc.

LEGUMES: All beans – including black, kidney, pinto, white, and chick peas – fall into this category, along with lentils, peas, and peanuts, including peanut butter. (I know! Sorry! I don't make the rules; I just share them.)

SOY: Soy is a legume, but I've called it out separately because it's insidious and can be found in unsuspected places, like cans of tuna. Soy is to be avoided in all its forms: edamame, tofu, meat substitutes, and food additives.

SUGAR: Sugar appears naturally in fruit, and you may eat fruit. Yay! But other natural sugars that are added to foods to sweeten them, like brown sugar, maple syrup, agave nectar, stevia, evaporated cane juice, and honey, are out. Also out are artificial sweeteners, like Splenda, Equal, Nutrasweet, and aspartame.

DAIRY: The source of milk doesn't matter – cow, sheep, or goat. Milk and the creamy things made from it are off our plates, including cream, butter, cheese, yogurt, and sour cream. Some paleo people eat grass-fed, full-fat dairy; for me, the negatives outweigh the pleasure.

ALCOHOL: There is no argument anywhere that alcohol makes us healthier. Plus, you have a drink, then your drink has a drink, and soon, you're face first in a pile of french fries with cheese sauce.

VEGETABLE OILS: This includes basic vegetable oil – which isn't made from vegetables at all! – as well as peanut, canola, sunflower, safflower, soybean, and corn oils.

Each of the No foods has its own unique properties that put it on that infamous list. Generally, these foods are excluded because they either produce blood sugar spikes, cause systemic inflammation, or both. Yes, some are so bad they both wreak havoc on your insulin levels and fire up your immune system. We very strongly dislike them. (We're looking at you, grains.)

So, there's potentially a lot of bad news in that list. I understand.

But I'm going to make you feel better right now...

Take a deep breath and think of every kind of meat, seafood, vegetable, and fruit you can.

Now think of fat sources like coconuts and avocados and olives and nuts and seeds. Visualize your list. Looks great, right? That's a lot of delicious food. And that is what makes up the paleo diet.

WE EAT REAL FOOD.
THE "YES" LIST

When I tell people I don't eat grains, sugar, or dairy, they invariably look at me like I've got two heads or as if I'm speaking Swahili, then they ask The Question: "What do you eat?!"

Animals and plants.

Generally speaking, the paleo diet is made up of nutrient-dense foods that began with dirt, rain, and sunshine. They come from the earth and would be recognizable as food by a person from any time in human history.

We eat real food: animal-based protein, vegetables, fruits, and natural fat sources.

ELK BISON VENISON GOAT RABBIT LAMB FIGS PEARS EGGS GRAPES CHICKEN APPLES
GOOSE TURKEY OSTRICH EMU SALMON HALIBUT DUCK
TUNA SHRIMP CLAMS MUSCLES SOLE TROUT TURNIPS
FLOUNDER LOBSTER TILAPIA BASS YAMS
SNAPPER MACKEREL SARDINES CASHEWS
ALMONDS PLUM BEEF COCONUT AVOCADO SUMMER
PEACHES ACORN SQUASH
POMEGRANATE STRAWBERRIES PINE NUTS ARTICHOKES ARUGULA BELL PEPPER SQUASH
OLIVES ASPARAGUS BEETS ORANGES PAPAYA NECTARINES SPINACH
BOK CHOY CABBAGE BRUSSELS BROCCOLI SWEET
SPROUTS CARROTS CELERY POTATO
CAULIFLOWER BUTTERNUT SQUASH
GARLIC COLLARD GREENS JICAMA CHARD CUCUMBERS EGGPLANT TURNIP
GREEN BEANS FENNEL
KALE PORK MUSTARD GREENS PARSNIPS GREENS
LEEKS MUSHROOMS OKRA ONIONS VEAL DATES
LETTUCE RED ONION RADISHES PUMPKIN
SCALLIONS SHALLOTS CRANBERRIES SNAP PEAS SNOW PEAS BLACKBERRIES
SPAGHETTI SQUASH APRICOTS BANANAS
ZUCCHINI CANTALOUPE LEMONS PEARS CHERRIES KIWI
WATER LIMES MELON
GRAPEFRUIT HONEYDEW RASPBERRIES MELON CRANBERRIES

I have excellent habits 95% of the time. I sleep eight hours per night to recover from and prepare for CrossFit training and lifting heavy barbells. I keep the house stocked with paleo ingredients and cook nutrient-infused food, so we can eat paleo food every day.

Then on rare occasions, I indulge. I become a temporary slug, and give in to the temptation of corn-based chip products, buttered popcorn, and an icy-cold glass of Prosecco. I might also occasionally sip on a glass of Ouzo and eat whipped cream.

These minor transgressions are possible because I make deposits in the good health bank the rest of the time. Every workout, every good night's sleep, every paleo meal is a deposit so that every once in a while, I can make withdrawals in the shape of a food treat.

This way of living started about two years ago when I made the switch to the paleo diet. Before then, I didn't have such excellent habits.

From grade school to the day I graduated from college, I was a chubby nerd and an easy target. My parents were both exceptionally good cooks – my dad owned a restaurant and my mom won almost every cooking contest she entered. I wore Sears "Pretty Plus" jeans because I really liked food, and I really didn't like to sweat. After a broken ankle and innumerable playground insults (At a bus stop, I was once unfavorably compared to a whale by one of the neighbor kids.), I stuck with reading and practicing the piano and roller skating to the library. I don't know how many gym classes I missed because I was "sick" or "forgot" my gym clothes. I do know that my P.E. attendance put my otherwise stellar grade point average in jeopardy.

Even though I avoided sports, I secretly admired the athletic kids. They walked taller than the rest of us. When I was in tenth grade, my dad took me to Annapolis to see the Navy band play a concert, and for about three weeks, I was determined to get in shape so I could apply to the Naval Academy. I abandoned that dream

because I was incapable of doing pushups and situps – and I was too embarrassed and overwhelmed to ask for help.

For most of my life, I was haunted by a deep desire to be different than I was. To be thin. To feel confident. To break the cycle of thinking of food – and my behavior – as "good" and "bad."

I joined Weight Watchers and became a Lifetime Member with a weight loss of more than 50 pounds. I signed up with a CrossFit gym and learned to love workouts that scared my socks off. But despite my successes, it was still my habit to celebrate and to grieve and to stress out and to relax with food.

Some day, I'd like to live in Prague. This is me, pretending to be a local, on our first visit to the Czech Republic in 2010.

Although I worked out regularly, I didn't feel as strong – inside or out – as I wanted to. I had insomnia and allergies and stomach aches. My body didn't feel like it belonged to me. Then in 2009, I learned I had a nodule on my thyroid. The risk of cancer was high, so I had the nodule surgically removed, and the doctor hoped that my remaining half-thyroid would continue to function. It held on for a few months, then stopped working. It was a very difficult time. It was like constantly having a case of the blues, and I was sluggish, foggy-headed, and desperately worried about re-gaining all the weight I'd worked so hard to lose.

Then I found Whole9.

It was surprisingly easy for me to give up grains, despite my deep affection for toast, but saying goodbye to my standard breakfast of blueberries with milk almost did me in. I did not approach the paleo rules with an open heart.

But I committed. I followed the eating guidelines. I made it a project to get eight hours of sleep **every night**. I worked with my doctor to find the right doses for my thyroid hormones. And finally, eventually, I got my body back.

I spent about three decades at war with my body, with my short legs and stocky frame and junk food cravings and emotional eating. In comparison, giving up grains and dairy was easy. And in return, I've forged a partnership with my body that uses good food as fuel.

Now I know when and how often I can indulge in non-paleo foods, and I enjoy those once-in-a-while treats like never before. The food tastes a lot better when it's savored and not followed by a chaser of self-recrimination. I finally know how to truly celebrate on special occasions, while I live clean and healthy the rest of the time.

Top: My husband Dave and I out for a run in Prague.

Bottom: The two of us at the Cowboy Breakfast, held every year before the opening of the rodeo in Austin, TX.

YOU KNOW HOW YOU COULD DO THAT?

Everyone in my family is a food lover. My dad is (mostly) Lebanese, and my mom is (mostly) Italian, with large families on both sides of the equation. Any gathering of the tribes included tables that buckled under the weight of homemade stuffed grape leaves and kibbeh on the Middle Eastern side – or homemade lasagna, meatballs, and cannoli at the Italian family reunions.

My family is happiest together in the kitchen. Cooking and the associated eating are the activities on which we all agree. We might go toe to toe on, say, the inherent value of my tattoos, but get us around a stove or a cutting board, and we are the very definition of collaboration. We move in a smooth rhythm, and the right ingredients seem to appear out of thin air. Suddenly, the clove of garlic I need has been perfectly minced, and somehow, the parsley is already chopped.

This harmony in the kitchen is the result of a lifetime of playing a game we call, "You Know How You Could Do That?"

It's generally played in a restaurant and goes like this:

The waiter places a gorgeous plate of food in front of someone – my mom, for example. I usually clap my hands with delight when the food arrives, and someone else – my dad, perhaps – says, "Oooh, that looks good."

Then Mom takes a bite. She smiles and nods her head. "Oh, yeah. That *is* good," she says.

The rest of us extend our forks and take a bite ourselves, nodding in agreement, making the appropriate, positive, nonverbal noises: *Mmmmm. Aaaaah. Oooooh.*

Then my dad will pause, tilt his head to the side, and maybe squint his eyes a little.

"It's really good, but… you know how you could do that?"

And then he'll offer a suggestion for a different spice or, perhaps, an added garnish. His idea will spark my imagination, so I'll take another bite from Mom's plate and offer a few suggestions of my own. Soon we've created variations that transform the chef's dish into something else entirely.

In recent years, we've adapted the game to be played with recipes, too. We don't even give the original chef the honor of trying the recipe as written. Instead, we go right into You Know How You Could Do That? mode and create our own version of the recipe.

Throughout this book, I've played You Know How You Could Do That? with my recipes, and I invite you to do the same. Have fun! Use your imagination! Make these recipes your own.

The kitchen has been my favorite hangout for a long time.

ABOUT THIS BOOK

THIS ISN'T A DIET BOOK OR A HEALTH BOOK

I know the word "paleo" in the title is probably what compelled you to choose this cookbook over others, which means you probably care about your health. I'm very glad! But my mission isn't to clobber you with the healthfulness of the recipes in this book. My mission is to inspire you with stories and tempt you with recipes that will make you want to smash in your face with joy.

I also want you to be healthy, so all of the recipes are free of gluten, grains, legumes, dairy, added sugars, and alcohol – and I've paid attention to things like Omega-6 and Omega-3 fatty acid ratios. I've worried about the somewhat annoying nutritional details so that you can just eat.

I want you to savor flavorful foods every time you eat, every single day. The majority of these recipes rely on meats, vegetables, fats, and spices to make your taste buds sing. When I've used calorie-dense foods like nuts or dried fruit, they act as condiments rather than primary ingredients.

THE CLOTHES MAKE THE GIRL

Many of the recipes in Well Fed *debuted on my blog,* **The Clothes Make The Girl**. *I started my blog in 2008 to write about my workout and fashion adventures. As my diet evolved to focus on paleo foods, I started to casually write about the things I was eating. Soon my adaptations of family recipes were some of the most popular pages on my site, and the idea for the cookbook started to simmer. I hope you'll visit The Clothes Make The Girl to learn more about me, CrossFit training, and strength training. Throughout* Well Fed, *I've included pointers to my blog for additional instruction, photos, and video demos, so you can play "You Know How You Could Do That?" online.*

JUST EAT

There's no nutritional information included with the recipes. If we eat real food, in quantities that are satiating, there's really no need to niggle over how many calories we ate and what percentage of them came from fat or carbohydrates. The recipes, however, don't go overboard, either. Fat is an essential nutrient for health and an important component for flavor, so my recipes include just enough fat to make them work, without being overindulgent.

When I adopted a paleo diet, I stopped thinking of foods as appropriate for breakfast, lunch, and dinner; instead, (say it with me) I just eat. Grilled chicken and vegetables make an excellent breakfast, and eggs with zucchini can be a comforting dinner after a tough day making your way in the world. Why would you deny yourself the fun of breakfast at 7:00 p.m. or steak after your morning workout by adhering to the conventional notions of breakfast, lunch, and dinner?

HOW TO USE THIS BOOK

The book is divided into three primary sections – The Paleo Kitchen, recipes, and Resources – to keep you well fed all week long. If you're an experienced cook or if a particular photo catches your eye, I know you'll probably be tempted to just start cooking, and I encourage you to do that!

But then I recommend that you return to the beginning of the book and read "The Weekly Cookup" to learn how to minimize your time in the kitchen and maximize the flavor of your food. The Weekly Cookup introduces the idea of "Hot Plates" and explains how I cook once to eat well all week.

Preparing quality food is among the most caring things we can do for ourselves and the people we love.

A VERY SPECIAL COOKBOOK

I didn't have much mad money when I was a student at Syracuse University. My parents generously paid for school, clothes, books, and other essentials, and I had a work study job (that often paid me even when I didn't show up 'cause I was too busy studying) to keep me stocked up on beer and non-dining hall food. I had plenty for which to be grateful, and I satisfied my book lust at the library.

When I moved into my own apartment, I went through an Italian cooking phase that taught me how to make homemade pesto and tomato, basil, and mozzarella salad; a Thai phase that required a trip to the Asian grocer for fresh lemongrass and other ingredients to make curry paste from scratch (My advice? Just buy the damn paste in a jar and make everything else yourself.); and an "I should eat beans instead of meat" phase.

On one trip to the library, I discovered *Middle Eastern Cooking* by Rose Dosti. Because of my dad's heritage, I grew up eating hummus, stuffed grape leaves, and lamb kabobs; and I had my dad's recipes for all of those things written on index cards in my kitchen cabinet. Dosti's cookbook expanded my repertoire with 192 pages of Greek, Arabic, Israeli, and North African recipes. I loved the cookbook so much that I wanted to buy it, but in the pre-internet world, it was impossible to find a copy.

The solution to the problem appeared when my dad came to visit one weekend. The two of us went to Kinko's and obsessively photocopied the whole thing. It took a long time, and we chatted and laughed while we plunked the book down on the glass, over and over, oohing and aahing at each recipe, and playing You Know How You Could Do That?

I bought a bright yellow cardboard expandable report cover, and that bootlegged cookbook traveled with me from Syracuse to an apartment in Escondido, California, to a houseboat in Sausalito to an apartment in San Francisco, and finally, to a duplex and now our house here in Austin. Last year, I found an original copy of the book on Amazon, but I couldn't bear to toss the photocopied version. I keep them both – side by side – on the bookshelf.

I've made the baba ghanoush and tahini dressing so many times that I don't need the cookbook to make them anymore. But every few months, I pull out Middle Eastern Cooking to make spiced olives or to drool over photos of a decadent Chicken Bastila (chicken, ground almonds, and cinnamon baked inside buttered philo dough and sprinkled with powdered sugar. I mean… really!), and I remember Dad and I, talking about nothing in particular while we broke several copyright laws simply to hold onto some wonderful, authentic recipes.

If you enjoy *Well Fed*, you can thank my dad for teaching me to love a well-constructed recipe for food that brings us together.

ABOUT THE RECIPES

I think playing in the kitchen is a pretty good time, so I've tried to make these recipes fun for you, too. Each recipe is packed with helpful tips, tasty nuggets of advice, and some silliness as a garnish. It is my fervent hope that you'll make these recipes your own. To do that, I recommend that you read through the recipe in its entirety at least once before you make it. Here are a few more tips to help ensure things come out just right.

HAPPY MEAT

If you have a kind heart, it's both a blessing and a curse to be at the top of the food chain. We have access to a wide variety of animal proteins, and I honor and respect those animals for making us stronger and healthier. Factory farming damages the environment and produces animals that are not optimally healthy, which means they also make us less healthy. Finances are always a concern, so I don't specify organic, grass-fed, pastured, wild-caught, or free-range protein in my recipes, but I do encourage you to buy the highest quality protein you can afford. If you can't invest in grass-fed meats, buy the leanest cuts you can find, remove excess fat before cooking, and drain the fat after cooking.

ORGANIC PRODUCE

It's best to eat local produce that's in season, both for the health of your body and your wallet. Sometimes I want eggplant in winter, even though it's not grown here that time of year. My recommendation is to buy local, organic versions of the produce identified by the Environmental Working Group as the "dirty dozen" (produce with high levels of pesticides). The list includes apples, bell peppers, blueberries, celery, cherries, grapes, kale (and other leafy greens), lettuce, nectarines, peaches, potatoes, and strawberries. For the rest of your produce needs, buy local, conventionally grown produce, and wash it well under running water to remove dirt and pesticides.

SERVING SIZES

I've included the number of servings in a recipe as a guide for planning, based on an "average" serving. For most people, a serving of protein is about four ounces and a serving of vegetables is about one cup. Keep this in mind if you're cooking for a giant, muscle-bound man or wee ones and adjust your quantity accordingly.

COOKING FATS

I'm no longer afraid of fat – it's an essential part of good health, and it's delicious. Double win! There's no reason, however, to go overboard either. My recipes include enough fat to appropriately cook and flavor the food. Feel free to increase the amount of fat if you'd like, but keep in mind that you will change the taste a bit if you reduce the fat.

For higher temperature cooking – like sautéing and baking – I recommend coconut oil, although some paleo eaters use clarified, organic, grass-fed butter or ghee instead. You can make that substitution in these recipes if you prefer. (All fats can be swapped with each other in a 1:1 ratio.) I do not recommend using olive oil for cooking; high heat causes olive oil to oxidize which has some health ramifications. Reserve olive oil for drizzling on already-cooked foods, salads, and homemade mayo.

SEASONING WITH SALT

American table salt is devoid of trace minerals; sea salt is a slightly superior option. Most sea salt, however, doesn't include the iodine found in table salt. I don't specify the type of salt to be used in these recipes, but I recommend iodized sea salt. All measurements refer to fine salt.

It's important to taste food for salt levels throughout the cooking process. Some of my recipes, where I think a particular amount makes it sing, specify the amount of salt, others simply say "salt and black pepper, to taste." I recommend that you season with salt during cooking and adjust seasonings again just before the end of cooking to get the best flavor. And with all spice quantities, feel free to adjust down or up according to taste.

COOKING TEMPERATURES
If you're using grass-fed meats, you'll get the best results if you use medium-high (or even medium) heat. High heat can make leaner, high-quality meat taste tough. You'll also notice that most of my recipes instruct you to preheat the pan before cooking; you'll be happiest if you don't ignore this advice.

WORKING WITH HOT PEPPERS
Some of these recipes include fresh jalapeños, which taste delicious, but can be hazardous to chop. When working with fresh jalapeños or other hot peppers, it's a good idea to either wear gloves or rub a little oil on the hand that's holding the pepper (but not the one holding the knife!) to protect yourself from the seeds and ribs. You can also burn a candle next to your cutting board to burn off the offending vapors or rub your hands with oil **after** chopping a hot pepper to remove the capsaicin residue. Absolutely, positively do not touch any part of your face while working with fresh hot peppers.

MIXING TOOLS
In most cases, my recipes instruct you to mix seasonings into raw meat by hand; this is primarily to save time. To make meatballs and sausages tenderer, blend the meat and seasonings in a food processor or mixer instead of by hand.

For stovetop cooking, I usually recommend a wooden spoon because it's versatile, durable, the handle doesn't (usually) get hot, and it won't scratch non-stick cookware.

OMITTING INGREDIENTS
In many of these recipes, garnish ingredients and some seasonings are listed as optional. Keep in mind that in all recipes, flavoring ingredients are always optional. Rather than skip an entire recipe if it includes something that's not on your list of favorites, just omit the element you don't like. None of these recipes will fail if you omit hot peppers or leave out the cumin.

NUTS AND DRIED FRUIT
When a *Well Fed* recipe includes nuts, seeds, or dried fruit, those ingredients are included as fun flavoring components, rather than primary ingredients. All nuts, seeds, and dried fruits included in these recipes are optional. If you're trying to minimize your Omega-6 fatty acids or fruit/sugar intake, you can omit the nuts and fruit without damaging the recipe.

MISE EN PLACE
(Chef-speak for "everything in place.") Prior to starting a recipe, set up like a cooking show: Measure and prep the ingredients you need to make the recipe, organize the equipment you need within easy reach, and pre-heat the oven or stove so you don't suddenly realize you need a diced onion when you've got your hands buried in a bowl of ground meat.

YOU'RE GONNA NEED A BIGGER BOWL
A few words of advice from my dad: Always, **always,** *always* use a bowl that's bigger than you think you need. (Thanks, Daddy!)

BETTER THAN A RESTAURANT

Once you know how to put paleo ingredients together, most restaurant food can't compete in terms of flavor. But there is something undeniably lovely about sitting down to a pretty table setting and having food served with flair. You can easily create a dining experience for yourself at home that rivals your favorite restaurant.

DON'T FORGET THE GARNISH

We eat first with our eyes, and restaurants do a bang-up job of making food look like something you'd want to eat. This one is so easy! Eating Pad Thai (p. 63)? Add a few chopped nuts and a wedge of lime to the plate. Staring at a pile of kale and ground beef? Drizzle it with Sunshine Sauce (p.45) and a sprinkle of chopped scallions. Edible garnishes not only pump up the flavor and add texture to your meals, but they give your eyes a feast, too.

A PLACE AT THE TABLE

Sometimes I like to plop on the couch with a bowl of food that I can slurp like an animal, and a few times a week, Dave and I use stools to casually sit at our kitchen island, instead of our big dining table. But most days, I set the table with placemats so that our brains register the message: "We're eating now." Take the time to slow down, chew your food, relax, and savor the flavors. It's an easy way to recreate the restaurant experience – and encourage the tradition of family dinner – at your dining table.

TABLEWARE

Fun and funky tableware doesn't need to be expensive to add a new dimension to home dining. I love to eat from my shallow bamboo bowl that's the perfect size for a Hot Plate (p. 35) or breakfast scramble, and we use polka dotted ice cream dishes for desserts like a handful of fresh cherries or Berries with Coconut Whipped Cream (p. 149). We picked up some inexpensive rice bowls and plastic chopsticks to make eating homemade Asian food just as much fun as takeout. Find a few plates that make your food look as good as it tastes. And why not serve yourself water in a wine glass, or place a wedge of lime on the rim of your club soda? You probably remember those small extras for guests; treat yourself like a guest, too.

MULTIPLE COURSES

Restaurants stretch out the dining experience by serving you in courses, so why not try the same at home? Relax and linger over a salad, then serve yourself the entrée after a brief interlude. It gives you more time for conversation and will leave you feeling more satiated than quickly eating your entire meal.

THE PALEO KITCHEN

Here's all the info you'll need to minimize the hassle of grocery shopping, to prep food so you're well fed all week long, and to make cooking a creative pleasure.

HOW TO: THE WEEKLY COOKUP

The film *Food, Inc.* changed our lives. It vividly drove home the detrimental effects of factory farming on the environment, our individual health, and the fabric of families. My husband Dave and I had already been eating paleo for about two months, but seeing that film guaranteed we'd never return to our old habits. We left the theater and drove directly to the grocery store, then spent hours reading labels and re-thinking how we were going to shop.

We made lists of what we could buy at a regular grocery store (pantry items, eggs, and produce) and what would require a trip to a higher-end store like Whole Foods or Sprouts (grass-fed, organic meat). We researched which produce should be organic and which could be conventionally grown. Then we stocked up on coconut aminos and loaded the freezer with grass-fed protein, so we wouldn't need to visit two grocery stores every week. We also signed up with a CSA (Community Supported Agriculture) for a weekly delivery of organic produce to supplement our trips to the store.

I'm not going to lie to you: At first, it was a huge annoyance. I was bitter. I complained a lot. But we both stuck to our guns, and soon it became routine. Our kitchen is now habitually stocked with healthy food, and it's not much more work than our previous, lazy, more destructive ways.

As the new shopping habits took hold, it became painfully evident that if we were going to take our health and longevity seriously, restaurant meals were not going to cut it.

I was going to be spending a lot of time in the kitchen.

For the first few weeks, I did. I felt like I was on an endless loop of chop, cook, eat, wash, repeat. It was tedious.

But then I remembered the lessons of my dad's restaurant kitchen and came up with a plan to keep us stocked with food, without driving myself mad. Now, just one big, weekly shopping trip and one Weekly Cookup keeps us happily fed all week.

I muster up about 30 meals and snacks each week: I eat a homemade breakfast every day except Saturday, and I pack my lunch and snacks for day job sustenance every weekday. To forage all the ingredients for that food, my husband does one giant shopping trip on Friday afternoons, and I spend about two hours on Sunday cooking for the week. With most of our food already cooked, meal prep on an average day takes about 30 minutes total: 10 minutes to pack my food for work and 20 minutes to throw together a delicious dinner.

I'm going to show you how to plan your own Weekly Cookups, so cooking can become one of your favorite things, too.

1. RUN YOUR KITCHEN LIKE A RESTAURANT

Most neighborhood restaurants don't cook every part of your meal to order. If they did, they'd never get the food to the table fast enough. Instead, restaurants do prep work for cooked food that divides the process into three broad categories:

- tastes best when eaten immediately: broiled or grilled meats, delicate produce
- tastes best after a day or two: casseroles, braised meats, stews and soups, sauces
- tastes great when partially cooked then caramelized in fat: many vegetables, some meats

Well Fed includes recipes that represent all three of these categories, so you can enjoy a variety of grab-and-go foods and slow-simmered meals throughout the week.

2. FEEL THE DIFFERENCE BETWEEN "COOKING" AND "MAKING DINNER"

Cooking is art, love, experimentation, relaxation, and fun. It can be savored as an experience. Sing along to music you love, while losing yourself in the rhythm of chopping and the aroma of far off places.

Making dinner is more like, "If I don't get that food from its ingredient state, into dinner state, and into my mouth soon, I'm going to murder someone."

I like to separate the two as much as possible. Cooking on Sunday is creative "me" time so that the rest of the week, making breakfast, lunch, and dinner is as painless as possible.

3. YOU WILL NEED A LOT OF FOOD

The increase in the amount of protein, vegetables, and fat you need to make the transition to paleo can be shocking. I was amazed at the sheer volume of veggies and meat we needed once we jettisoned cheese, tortillas, toast, pasta, and rice. You know how you used to find wilted, moldy vegetables in the back of your crisper drawer? Those days are over; you are now a veggie-eating machine. Buy accordingly.

COOKING WOD

In CrossFit, the workout of the day (WOD) is always timed. The idea is that you do the movements as quickly and efficiently as possible, without sacrificing form and technique. It's very motivating and on many occasions, the clock inspires me to do things I don't think I can do.

One day, feeling unenthusiastic about the assembly line of meat and vegetable prep on my schedule, I decided to treat my Sunday Cookup like a WOD. Could I do all my food prep in one hour?

I set a stopwatch for 60:00 and got busy rattling some pots and pans. I bounced back and forth among the oven, the stove – where I had two pans going at once – and the gas grill outside the kitchen door. My iPod cranked out appropriate cooking tunes. (For me, that's Social Distortion, The Clash, and Duran Duran, with a little Barry Manilow thrown into the mix.) I set a second timer to beep at five-minute intervals so I wouldn't burn anything.

SUNDAY COOKING WOD
For time, 60-minute cutoff:
Steam-sauté a head of bok choy (p. 33)
Steam-sauté a head of Swiss chard
Roast a large spaghetti squash (p. 123)
Roast sweet potatoes
Chop cauliflower for pilaf (p. 121)
Grill 2 1/2 pounds chicken thighs (p. 29)
Grill 1 pound chicken sausage
Stew lamb for Rogan Josh (p. 85)
Brown 2 pounds ground beef (p. 31)
Boil 1 dozen eggs
Mix pork and seasonings for Scotch Eggs (p. 83)

My time: 61:00 / **Cleanup time:** 5:00

Think you don't have time to prepare food so you can eat clean all week? I call bull on that! One hour of chopping, steaming, stewing, mixing, and grilling netted me enough raw materials to build meals for at least five days. Granted, it wasn't one of those fun and leisurely cooking experiences, but every workout at the gym isn't an endorphin-laced funfest, either. Sometimes, for your own good, you've just got to get it done.

OUR WEEKLY HAUL

The list below is a pretty good representation of what we eat in a typical week. Keep these stats in mind as you read the list:

1. Dave is 6'5" and weighs about 250. I'm 5'4" and 150 pounds of fury. I eat between 1700-1800 calories a day: 40% fat, 30% protein, 30% carbs. Dave eats more than that!

2. We usually eat out in restaurants only once or twice a week. During the weekdays, we cook breakfast and dinner at home. I pack my lunch and snacks to take to work; Dave eats lunch at the house.

3. We shop at a regular grocery store and a natural foods store. We also get a weekly organic produce delivery and order grass-fed meat online or from a local meat share.

PROTEIN	FAT
2 pounds turkey sausage	3/4 jar coconut oil
3 pounds chicken thighs	1/2 bottle olive oil
2 pounds chicken breasts	1 pound cashews
2 pounds ground lamb	(Dave likes to snack on these a lot!)
3 dozen eggs	
2 pounds turkey bacon	
2 pounds ground beef	

PRODUCE

3 pounds green beans	1 head red cabbage
4 green bell peppers	1 pound Brussels sprouts
1 pound okra	5 oranges
2 pints grape tomatoes	2 apples
4 carrots	2 pink grapefruits
2 pounds snap peas	4 sweet potatoes
8 cucumbers	1/2 pound baby carrots
2 eggplants	3 onions
3 heads cauliflower	2 heads garlic
1 head green cabbage	1 bunch flat-leaf parsley

4. YOU WILL NEED A LOT OF STORAGE CONTAINERS

Stock up on containers with tight-fitting lids in sizes ranging from small enough for a handful of snap peas to large enough for half a casserole. You are now in the business of making your own packaged food, and you need high-quality packaging.

5. BUILD A PROTEIN FOUNDATION

Protein is key, so build your meals from the protein up. I grill a few pounds of chicken, brown a few pounds of ground meat, and boil a dozen eggs every week, so we have the protein building blocks we need to create meals quickly.

Cooked meat can be served "diner style" with veggies on the side or diced for a stir-fry, simmered in a quick coconut milk curry, or turned into sautés with exotic seasonings. (I call these Hot Plates; see page 35.) Toss in an egg for extra protein, or construct a giant omelet.

Here's a simple formula to help you calculate how much protein you need to buy for the week:

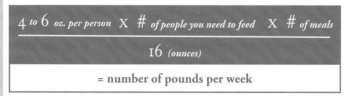

$$\frac{4 \text{ to } 6 \text{ oz. per person} \times \# \text{ of people you need to feed} \times \# \text{ of meals}}{16 \text{ (ounces)}}$$

= number of pounds per week

Example:
4 ounces x Mel x 20 meals = 80 ounces / 16
= 5 pounds of protein + extra for snacks

6 ounces x Dave x 20 meals = 120 ounces / 16
= 7.5 pounds of protein + extra for snacks

So, Dave and I chow our way through the equivalent of approximately 13 pounds of protein each week, just in our main meals.

6. PREP YOUR VEGETABLES

We eat a lot of fresh veggies every day, but I prepare most of them in advance. I chop and steam-sauté a variety of veggies (p. 33), like cabbage, broccoli, bell peppers, green beans, and leafy greens so they're ready to be sautéed with seasonings and fat.

Heartier vegetables like Brussels sprouts and spaghetti squash are roasted in the oven for quick reheating when we're ready to eat. Cauliflower is chopped in the food processor so it's ready to be turned into Cauliflower Pilaf (p. 121), and veggies we like to eat raw – lettuce, bell peppers, snap peas, jicama, and cucumbers – are washed and stored in the fridge so they're ready to be eaten.

I always have chopped, frozen broccoli, cauliflower, spinach, and collard greens in the freezer. They have the same nutrient profile as fresh (sometimes even better) and go from frozen to ready to eat in under 10 minutes.

Based on the idea that each of your meals will include at least two different vegetables and that your snacks will also include about one or two cups of veggies each, **you need about eight to ten cups of veggies per person per day.** A cucumber yields about two cups, a red pepper is about one cup, and a handful of snap peas is about a cup. Fear not! You'll get pretty good at eyeballing the right amounts at the store, and you cannot overeat vegetables, so dig in.

7. RELY ON HOT PLATES

More than half of the meals we eat every week are Hot Plates (p. 35): Meals we build spontaneously from raw materials like grilled chicken, browned ground meat, steam-sautéed veggies, and sauces. Our pre-dinner conversation usually goes like this:

Me: *Are you in the mood for Chinese, Middle Eastern, Mexican, or Italian?*
Dave: *Mmmm... Mexican!*
Me: *Beef or chicken?*
Dave: *Beef!*

Then I pull the containers of ground beef and steam-sautéed peppers and cabbage from the fridge. While they're warming up in the pan with a little fat, I turn homemade mayo into Southwestern Cumin-Lime Dressing (p. 59) to drizzle on top of our Mexican Hot Plate, and we're eating dinner in about 10 minutes from fridge to table.

Hot Plates should make up the majority of your meals. They're fast, they're nutritious, and if you alternate them with "real recipes," you will naturally eat a balance of Omega-3 and Omega-6 fats, plenty of vegetables, a wide variety of protein sources, and your taste buds will never get bored. Find step-by-step instructions and tons of ideas for Hot Plates on page 35.

8. TRY A FEW RECIPES

Each week, in addition to the basics, I cook two or three "real recipes" that require me to follow instructions or invest a little more time. Things like Italian Sausage & Eggplant Strata (p. 101) or Shepherd's Pie (p. 97) or Chocolate Chili (p. 73) are complete meals and taste better after a day or two in the fridge. They require no additional work beyond a reheat, so they're the perfect cooking and "making dinner" experience.

To summarize, here's a formula for your Weekly Cookup:
[raw materials for Hot Plates] + [2-3 recipes] + random snacks

SUPER SNACK

Every week, I eat almost the same snacks every day. That way, when I go shopping, I know I need to buy a bunch of X.

For example, one of my favorite snacks is what I call an "Antipasto Snack Pack." It's composed of a handful of snap peas, half a red pepper cut into strips, and half a cucumber sliced into coins, plus a handful of black olives, a piece of cold grilled chicken, and a little dill pickle.

To make shopping easier, I calculate how much of the ingredients I need to make it every day for five days – two bags of snap peas, three red peppers, three cucumbers, two cans of olives – and automatically add those to my shopping list every week.

Sometimes I go a little crazy, and I do something daring like use green bell pepper instead of red or swap carrots for the snap peas. This limited spontaneity ensures that I don't get bored, and the consistent veggies mean I don't suffer a 6:00 a.m. realization that I don't have food to pack for a work snack. The added bonus is that I also know I'm hitting good nutrition, because I've got a variety of veggies, solid protein, and quality fat in each snack pack.

A SAMPLE WEEKLY COOKUP

Here's an example list of the foods I prep during my Sunday Cookup so we can make Hot Plates all week:

2-3 pounds Basic Grilled Chicken Thighs (p. 29)
2-3 pounds Basic Ground Meat (p. 31)
1 large cabbage, steam-sautéed (p.33)
1 large spaghetti squash, roasted (p. 123)
1 large cauliflower, riced in the food processor (p. 121)
2 pounds green beans, steam-sautéed
1 dozen hard-boiled eggs
1-2 jicama, peeled and cut into matchsticks
Olive Oil Mayo (p. 43)
1-2 supplemental veggies cooked "to order:"
  fennel
  baby spinach
  cucumbers
  carrots
  snap peas
  bell peppers

PLUS, I ALWAYS HAVE THESE THINGS IN THE PANTRY AND FREEZER:
tuna, packed in olive oil
sardines, boneless, skinless, packed in olive oil
kipper snacks
olives
coconut milk
frozen chopped spinach or collard greens
frozen chopped broccoli
frozen cauliflower florets
frozen baby Brussels sprouts
frozen shrimp

Plus, we get our organic produce delivery filled with surprises that I use for inspiration: "Oh, look! Lots of eggplant! I can make Baba Ghanoush!" (p. 139)

See page 21 for a complete list of essential goodies to keep stocked in your pantry.

YOUR PALEO PANTRY

Paleo eating is basically about animal protein, piles of fresh produce, and quality fat sources. But there's more to it than that. Those ingredients are the foundation, but with a well-stocked pantry, you can turn raw materials into meals, every day of the week.

SPICE IT UP!

One of the things I love about spices and other seasonings is that, much like a good book, they can take you just about anywhere in the world. When I mixed up a batch of tuna with lemon, black olives, mint, and piquant peppers, I was no longer in hot and humid Austin, Texas. For just a little while, I was on holiday, along the sunny coast of the Mediterranean, enjoying a light lunch before a jaunt along the coast on a scooter (wearing a really cute sundress, giant sunglasses, and a scarf in my hair).

INDIVIDUAL SPICES & HERBS

Here are the individual spices that appear in my recipes most often. If you have these at your disposal, you should have what you need to make lots of tasty recipes. Don't feel like you need to buy them all at once, but I encourage you to slowly build your collection as you explore new recipes. An unfamiliar spice or herb can open up a whole new world of flavor.

Bay Leaf: Adds depth to soups, stews, and braises, especially in Mediterranean cuisine. According to legend, the oracle at Delphi chewed bay leaves to promote her visions.

Cardamom: A key ingredient in Indian curries.

Cayenne Pepper: Adds a little to heat to just about anything. Named for the city of Cayenne in French Guiana.

Chives, dried: Used in French and Swedish cooking, these are the smallest species of edible onion with a mild flavor. Ideal for scrambled eggs, steamed veggies, and creamy salad dressings, I throw them into everything!

Cinnamon: A must-have basic for sweet and savory foods in just about every ethnic cuisine. In ancient times, it was prized as a gift fit for the gods.

Cloves: Used in sweets, as well as Indian, Vietnamese, Mexican, and Dutch cooking. Eaten on their own, cloves will numb your tongue!

Cocoa: A rich surprise in savory dishes like chili. Hello, **chocolate**!

Coriander, ground: Common in Middle Eastern, Asian, Mediterranean, Indian, Mexican, Latin American, African, and Scandinavian foods. Coriander is the seed of the cilantro plant.

Cumin, ground: Essential for North African, Middle Eastern, Mexican, and some Chinese dishes. The Greeks used cumin at the table as a seasoning and that habit continues in modern Morocco. My favorite spice!

Garlic Powder, granulated: For just about everything. Fresh is best for cooking, but homemade spice blends require dried garlic, and I'm not going to lie to you: Sometimes I just reach for the powder when I don't feel like dealing with mincing the fresh cloves. I'm a culinary pragmatist.

Ginger, ground: A necessity for Indian curries and Asian dishes. Scrambled with eggs, it's a paleo home remedy for a cough.

Mint, dried: A magical flavor in Middle Eastern and Mediterranean cooking.

Mustard Seed, ground: Used in homemade mayo, salad dressings, and piquant spice blends. Jewish texts compare the knowable universe to the size of a mustard seed to teach humility.

Oregano: The "pizza herb" for everything Italian. It's also tasty in Turkish, Syrian, Greek, and Latin American foods.

Paprika: Adds a peppery bite and rich color to Moroccan, Middle Eastern, and Eastern European dishes.

Pepper, black: Important for just about everything. Buy it whole and crush just before using for optimal flavor.

Red Pepper, crushed: Made from a variety of dried hot red peppers. Adds zip to Italian and Asian dishes.

Sea Salt: Salt brings out the best in everything we eat. I like fine sea salt for cooking, preferably iodized.

Thyme, dried: Used in Middle Eastern, Indian, Italian, French, Spanish, Greek, Caribbean, and Turkish cuisines. The ancient Greeks believe thyme was a source of courage.

SPICE BLENDS

This book includes recipes for some spice blends – like Italian Sausage Seasoning and Pizza Seasoning (both on p.49) – that often include sugar when they're commercially produced. For other international flavors that I don't need to make myself, I rely on top-notch spice shops. My favorites are Penzeys Spices and the Savory Spice Shop; find their contact info in Resources (p. 156).

Chili Powder: Used in Tex-Mex, Indian, Chinese, and Thai. A blend of chili peppers, cumin, oregano, garlic, and salt. Heat varies based on the type of chilies used.

Chinese Five-Spice Powder: Balances the yin and yang in Chinese food with star anise, Szechuan peppercorns, cinnamon, cloves, and fennel seeds. In Hawaii, it's used as a condiment in a table-top shaker.

Curry Powder: Essential for curries, egg or tuna salad, and vegetable dishes. My favorite is Penzeys salt-free Maharajah Style Curry Powder.

Greek Seasoning: Mixed into beef or lamb, it tastes like gyro meat. Blended with olive oil and lemon juice, it's salad dressing and marinade. Stirred into homemade mayo, it's Greek dipping sauce.

Italian Herb Mix: Essential for my homemade Creamy Italian Salad Dressing (p. 59) and enormously helpful for providing a taste of Italy to vegetables, soups, stews, and sautés.

Tsardust Memories (Penzeys Spices): Spicy, not hot, and mildly sweet, when it's mixed into ground pork or beef, it creates instant Eastern European sausage. It's also wonderful as a rub for roasted or grilled meat or sprinkled onto hearty vegetables like cabbage and winter squashes.

Turkish Seasoning (Penzeys Spices): Blended into ground beef or lamb, it creates instant Mediterranean kebabs, is also tasty as a rub on grilled meats, and is lovely scrambled into eggs and veggies.

Za'atar: A classic Middle Eastern finishing seasoning – made from sesame seeds, dried sumac, salt, and thyme – to sprinkle on salads and cooked vegetables.

OTHER PANTRY ESSENTIALS

These items are always in my cabinet and on my weekly shopping list so I never run out. They easily transform the mundane into the memorable.

Coconut Aminos: Almost identical to soy sauce in taste, coconut aminos are a healthy replacement for Asian-inspired recipes.

Coconut Oil: Use organic, unrefined coconut oil for optimal health benefits. It lends a somewhat buttery flavor to dishes and can be used at high temperatures without oxidizing (which means it remains good for you, even if you turn up the heat). Because it's saturated, it's solid at cooler temperatures, so it's a good stand-in for butter in baked treats.

Coconut Flakes, unsweetened: Eaten on their own or sprinkled into and on top of dishes, coconut flakes add another dimension of flavor and texture.

Coconut Milk: Equally at home in sweet and savory dishes, it's an excellent replacement for heavy cream or yogurt in curries and sauces. According to Whole9, it's okay if the ingredient list includes guar gum, but avoid brands that include sulfites or added sugar.

Dried Fruit: Because it's naturally high in sugar, I don't snack on dried fruit, but a few dates, raisins, or dried cranberries can add just the right touch of sweetness to savory foods. I keep a small amount in the cabinet (just enough to flavor my food but not to feed the sugar demons). Be sure to look for varieties without added ingredients.

Extra-Virgin Olive Oil: Fruity with a peppery kick at the end, EVOO is best for salads and finishing cooked dishes. For high temperature cooking, use coconut oil.

Light-flavored Olive Oil: Less expensive and less flavorful, use this type of olive oil for Olive Oil Mayo (p. 43).

Olives: A salty, chewy addition to salads, snacks, and garnishes, olives also add a dose of healthy fats. Again, check ingredient labels for added junk; you want only water, olives, and salt.

Nuts: I try not to snack on nuts, but instead save them for adding crunchy flavor to cooked foods. I keep a small amount of pine nuts, dry-roasted unsalted almonds, pecans, and cashews on hand.

Pickles, Banana Peppers, Jalapeños: These crispy, piquant nibbles transform salads and sautés from ho-hum to yum. Jalapeños are Dave's favorite addition to egg scrambles.

Beef and Chicken Broth: Look for organic chicken, beef, and vegetable stock that doesn't contain any added sugar, starches, or soy. Or, even better, make your own!

Sunbutter and/or Almond Butter: A healthier alternative to peanut butter, get sugar-free varieties that include only seeds or nuts and salt, then prepare for lusciousness.

Tomatoes, Tomato Paste: For quick sauces and to add depth to soups, stews, and sautés, tomatoes are like a secret weapon. Look for brands that contain only tomatoes and salt. I recommend all of the Muir Glen varieties and especially like the fire roasted options.

Tuna, Sardines, Kipper Snacks: Good-to-go protein that requires no fridge or cookery. Read the labels to make sure it's pure.

IN THE FREEZER

Many dinnertime meltdowns have been averted by reaching into the freezer for some quick-thaw protein and vegetables. Frozen veggies are just as nutritious as fresh, so stock up for food-related emergencies. Always in my freezer:

WILD-CAUGHT, COOKED SHRIMP

CHOPPED SPINACH

CHOPPED COLLARD GREENS

CHOPPED BROCCOLI

CAULIFLOWER FLORETS

FRENCH-CUT GREEN BEANS

THE PERFECT BOWL

For as long as I can remember, what we call the "Sitti bowl" has been the most important tool in our kitchen. It's a 4-quart Pyrex bowl, yellow on the outside, white on the inside.

"Sitti" means grandmother in Arabic, and we call this the Sitti bowl because my mom inherited it from my great-grandmother – my Sitti – in 1970. As the story goes, my parents had recently moved into the house where I grew up on East Mifflin Street in Orwisburg, Pennsylvania. Sitti had come to their new house to teach my mom how to make Syrian bread. (You probably know it as pita, but in our house, it always has been, and always will be, Syrian bread.) At the time, my mom didn't have a bowl large enough to knead the dough, so Sitti gave my mom the big yellow bowl that day, and that's how the Sitti bowl came to be.

I don't know how much I actually remember of my Sitti, because she died when I was very little. My dad's stories about her, along with the few photos I've seen of her with coiffed 1940s hair and house dresses, have implanted memories deep in my heart and my head.

According to legend, she removed hot pies from the oven without oven mitts and could be found on the back porch smoking cigars, while Syrian bread puffed in the oven. I think her days in the old country – and her new life in America – must have been pretty tough. To me, she represents the best that we can be: A no-nonsense person who wouldn't be pushed around, but who could be very loving and nurturing at just the right moments.

Sitti taught my parents how to make Lebanese food, and they taught me. When we cooked together – stuffed grape leaves and spinach pies and hummus and kibbeh – we did all the work

in that yellow bowl. It's not only the perfect size for mixing or tossing, it immediately infuses love into everything prepared in it.

When my husband Dave and I lived in San Francisco, we found a clone of the Sitti bowl in a vintage store in the Mission, and it has held a special place in my kitchen ever since. It is also known as the Sitti bowl and is treated with reverence: hand-washed only and preferred over the glass nesting bowls from Williams-Sonoma.

Now that I spend so much time in the kitchen, the right tools have become even more important to me. I need to feel like the tools and I are working together to create nourishing, soul-feeding food. If you're beginning to cook or expanding your repertoire, I encourage you to find the tools you like the best and invest in the ones that make cooking both easier and more pleasurable, because the first step toward eating well is cooking well.

This is my Sitti. Her real name was Edith! My paternal Nana and Pop Pop sit to her right.

RECOMMENDED EQUIPMENT

With these basics, you should be able to make everything in this cookbook. For my recommendations on specific pieces of equipment, along with buying information, visit www.theclothesmakethegirl.com/store.

Large Cutting Board: Almost every recipe begins with chopping, and a hefty cutting board protects the knife, your countertop, and you.

A Really Good Knife: In the kitchen, your knife is an extension of you. Choose a knife that feels comfortable in your hand. I like an 8-inch blade; it works well on both meat and produce.

Food Processor or Blender: Essential for the sauces and seasonings that make paleo food sing, a food processor is a solid investment in your healthy, happy taste buds. You can get away with either a processor or blender, but I have both, and I'm glad.

Chili Pot: Get a pot larger than you think you need, preferably with a non-stick interior and a heavy bottom.

Large Sauté Pan: Essential for everyday cooking, invest in a non-stick, 12-inch skillet, so it's large enough to handle Hot Plates with ease.

Large Baking Sheets: Insulated sheets help prevent burning and a rim prevents smoke-inducing drips inside the oven. Ideally, you should have at least two of these.

Sturdy Mixing Bowls: Graduated sizes ensure you have a Sitti bowl for large kneading projects and spice-sized bowls to keep your workspace tidy.

Colander or Wire Sieve: For washing produce, draining steamed foods or fatty meats, and sweating raw vegetables.

Assorted Baking Pans: You can get by with either a 13X9 or two 8- or 9-inch round pans, but if you have both, you have more options. Buy them at thrift stores or yard sales and stock up.

Julienne Peeler: Transforms raw zucchini, yellow squash, and cucumbers into noodles in a flash.

Standing or Hand Mixer: You can get by with just a food processor, but a mixer can handle more volume and more delicate tasks, like whipping coconut milk into luscious dessert topping.

Measuring Cups & Spoons: You'll have everything you need if you invest in a 2-cup liquid measuring cup, dry measuring cups ranging in size from 1 cup to 1/4 cup, and measuring spoons from 1 tablespoon to 1/4 teaspoon.

Rubber Scraper: I don't like to leave even one drop of homemade mayo inside the blender! Look for a scraper that's both sturdy and flexible, so it bends into corners.

Parchment Paper and/or Aluminum Foil: Invaluable for minimizing clean-up time. I prefer having both on hand, but if you must choose one, go with aluminum foil.

Storage Containers: Essential for stocking up on paleo ingredients. You'll need more than you think, and there is acute satisfaction in a fridge filled with ingredients and homemade food.

Wooden Spoons: My preferred tool for sautéing, mixing, and tossing.

Garlic Press: Not required, but a real time saver unless you're adept at mincing with a knife.

Pastry or Barbecue Brush: Cheap to buy and priceless in the kitchen for adding the finishing touch to your homemade dishes.

Kitchen Shears: A huge timesaver for prepping raw meat, cleaning produce, and mincing fresh herbs.

Tongs: Essential for grilling and browning meat for stews.

Skewers, Metal or Bamboo: Minimize the fuss of grilling small items, plus: Meat on a stick! Soak bamboo skewers in water for 30 minutes before using to prevent burning.

Grater/Zester: You're not grating cheese anymore, but citrus zest is a magical ingredient.

THE WEEKLY COOKUP

These simple recipes and instructions will help you create delicious, international Hot Plates from simple, nourishing, and tasty ingredients.

The caramelized, charred bits are my favorite. They add depth and texture that elevate a simple sauté to meal status.

SERVES 6 to 8

PREP	COOK
05 MIN.	10 MIN.

Fresh off the grill, this chicken is crisp and garlicky with a satisfying char. Dressed up with seasonings, sauces, and vegetables, the leftovers are so versatile, they're easily transformed from "basic ingredient" to a meal worthy of licking your plate clean.

INGREDIENTS

- 2 pounds boneless, skinless chicken thighs
- salt
- ground black pepper
- coarse (granulated) garlic powder
- paprika

DIRECTIONS

Preheat a gas grill with all burners on high and the lid closed, about 10 minutes.

Place the chicken on a large platter or baking sheet in a single layer, smooth side facing up. Sprinkle generously with salt, pepper, and garlic powder, then add just enough paprika for a little kick. Flip the chicken and season the other side.

Place the chicken smooth side down on the heated grill and close the lid. Cook 4-5 minutes, then flip and cook an additional 4 minutes with the lid closed. The chicken is cooked when the juices run clear, and it has turned toasty brown on both sides.

YOU KNOW HOW YOU COULD DO THAT?

No grill? Preheat the oven to 400 F. Follow seasoning instructions for grilling then place the chicken in a single layer, smooth side up, in a large baking dish. Bake 30-35 minutes until juices run clear and the tops are well browned.

TASTY IDEAS

HOT PLATES, P. 35
PAD THAI, P. 63
BBQ PORK FRIED RICE, P. 93

NOTES

This works for boneless chicken breasts and pork chops, too. Brush meat with melted coconut oil before seasoning and reduce grill time to 4 minutes per side.

Grass-fed meats prefer low, slow temps, so turn down the heat and let the meat relax into the browning process.

SERVES 6 to 8

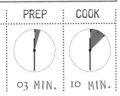

PREP · COOK
03 MIN. · 10 MIN.

A pan of freshly-browned ground meat is pure potential, a culinary blank canvas. Sometimes, the aroma is so tempting, I eat it just like that – with a spoon, from a bowl – so I can experience the pure meat-ness of it. Later, combined with vegetables and the right seasonings, this basic can be elevated to luscious international status.

INGREDIENTS

1 tablespoon coconut oil

1 medium onion, diced (about 1 cup)

2 pounds ground meat (beef, bison, lamb, pork, turkey, or chicken)

salt

ground black pepper

coarse (granulated) garlic powder

DIRECTIONS

Heat a large skillet over medium-high heat, about 3 minutes. Add coconut oil and allow it to melt. Toss the onion in the pan and sauté, stirring with a wooden spoon. Cook until crisp-tender and translucent, about 5 minutes.

Crumble the ground meat into the pan with your hands, then break up large chunks using the wooden spoon. Season generously with salt, pepper, and garlic powder. Continue to cook and stir until the meat has no pink spots and reaches a warm brown hue, about 7-10 minutes. If you're not using grass-fed meat, drain the excess fat before you dig in.

YOU KNOW HOW YOU COULD DO THAT?

Meat combos can be fun! Good pairings include pork+beef, beef+turkey, beef+lamb, and chicken+turkey.

TASTY IDEAS

HOT PLATES, P. 35
EGG FOO YONG, P. 87
JICAMA HOMEFRIES, P. 131

NOTES

Ever notice that a cast-iron skillet is not only the ideal kitchen tool, it can also double as a weapon?

Taste the rainbow! Be sure to eat a variety of veggies every week and strive for a mix of bright green, red, purple, and orange.

STEAM-SAUTÉED VEGGIES

SERVES *a lot*

PREP	COOK
05 MIN.	3–7 MIN.

Most days, I eat vegetables at breakfast, lunch, dinner, and snacks. That's in the neighborhood of six or seven cups of veggies every day. Oh, there's so much chopping and cooking! So once a week, I turn into a Veg-O-Matic and make it my mission to clean and partially steam at least three different vegetables, so they're ready to be transformed into meals when I need them.

INGREDIENTS

your favorite vegetables

water

DIRECTIONS

Wash your veggies under running water, then, using a sharp knife, cut or slice into desired shape, depending on your mood and tastes. It's best if you keep the pieces roughly the same size, so they'll cook evenly.

Heat a large skillet over medium-high heat. Toss the still-wet-from-the-washing vegetable into the pan, cover with a lid, and allow the residual water to soften the veg a bit. Remove the lid, and stir vigorously with a wooden spoon until the vegetable is softened but not completely cooked. If the veg sticks to the pan or begins to brown, add a tablespoon of water to continue the steaming process.

Place each vegetable in its own container and store in the fridge. Be sure to pop the containers into the refrigerator while hot – cooling at room temperature allows bacteria to grow. I usually reserve the bottom shelf of my fridge for hot veggies.

When it's time to eat, heat about 1-2 teaspoons of coconut oil in your skillet, then toss in the partially-cooked veggies and seasonings. No fuss, no muss, no chopping right before dining!

This method works best for fibrous, sturdy vegetables. Tender veggies like snap peas, snow peas, fennel, asparagus, and spinach are best cooked "to order."

YOU KNOW HOW YOU COULD DO THAT?

Need ideas? This is a short list of vegetables that are good choices to have around for everyday fortification – and they're hearty enough to stand up to this kind of pre-cooking:

BELL PEPPER, SLICED

BOK CHOY, CHOPPED

BRUSSELS SPROUTS, CUT IN HALF

BROCCOLI, BROKEN INTO FLORETS

CABBAGE (RED OR GREEN), SLICED OR CHOPPED

CARROTS, SLICED

CAULIFLOWER, BROKEN INTO FLORETS

CELERY, SLICED THIN

CHARD, CHOPPED

COLLARD GREENS, CHOPPED

EGGPLANT, SLICED OR CHOPPED

GREEN BEANS, WHOLE

KALE, CHOPPED

MUSTARD GREENS, CHOPPED

PARSNIPS, SLICED

TURNIP GREENS, CHOPPED

YELLOW SQUASH, SLICED

ZUCCHINI, SLICED

TASTY IDEAS PLATES, P. 35

These are the ingredients for one of my favorite Hot Plates: ground beef, Roasted Spaghetti Squash (p. 123), and red cabbage sautéed in coconut oil with garlic, parsley, and Penzeys Tzardust Memories. For breakfast, I also add one scrambled egg.

PREP | COOK
05 MIN. | 10 MIN.

This is not so much a recipe as it is a formula for putting together meals from protein, veggies, and a world of spices and seasonings. We eat these sautés for more than half of our meals every week. With this approach, you can make the transition from "cold ingredients" to "delicious meal" in under 10 minutes, and it's an easy way to satisfy an "I'm really in the mood for [insert name of ethnic food here]" craving.

INGREDIENTS

Per person:

1/2 tablespoon coconut oil

1/4 medium onion, diced (about 1/4 cup)

1 clove garlic, minced (about 1 teaspoon)

3-6 ounces of cooked protein (p. 29 and 31)

2 cups Steam-Sautéed Veggies (p. 33)

salt and black pepper, to taste

spices

NOTES

DIRECTIONS

Heat a large skillet over medium-high heat, about 3 minutes. Add coconut oil and allow it to melt. Toss the onion and garlic in the pan and sauté, stirring with a wooden spoon. Cook until crisp-tender and translucent, about 5 minutes.

Add the spices to the pan and stir until fragrant, about 30 seconds. Add the protein and vegetables, sprinkle generously with salt and pepper. Stir continuously with a wooden spoon until it's hot and the vegetables begin to brown, about 5 minutes.

YOU KNOW HOW YOU COULD DO THAT?

Really in a hurry? Feeling particularly lazy? Skip the onion and garlic step and proceed straight to "meat in pan." The flavors will have a little less depth, but your meal will still be tasty. You can also amp up the protein and breakfast quotient by adding 1-2 scrambled eggs along with the protein and vegetables.

THE FORMULA

PER PERSON =

3-6 OUNCES OF PROTEIN

+ 2 CUPS VEG

+ 1 TABLESPOON FAT

+ SEASONINGS

GET LOTS OF HOT PLATES IDEAS OVER HERE ▶

HOT PLATES MANGEZ! ESSEN! EAT!

You really can't go wrong by following your taste buds, but I've listed some combos that work particularly well together. Traditional ethnic cuisines are delicately nuanced and are influenced by geographical region and the whims of the cook. These ingredient recommendations are merely broad strokes at recreating the predominant flavors of each cuisine.

NOTE: For grilled meats, see Grilled Chicken Thighs (p. 29), and for ground meats, see the recipe for Garlic-Browned Ground Meat (p. 31).

AMERICAN

You can always make yourself a "Diner Dinner:" load up a plate with protein, two veggie sides, and a salad. Or make a Hot Plate with all-American meat and "potatoes."

ground beef
Jicama Home Fries (p. 131), bell pepper

CHINESE

It's also not a bad idea to scramble an egg with one teaspoon coconut aminos and throw that in the pan near the end of cooking time. Serve on a bed of Basic Cauliflower Rice (p. 121). Garnish with toasted sesame seeds, chopped scallions, and/or one teaspoon of sesame oil. You can find the Best Stir Fry Sauce Ever on page 51.

ground beef
eggplant, red bell pepper
Best Stir Fry Sauce Ever

ground beef
broccoli, slivered carrots, mushrooms
Best Stir Fry Sauce Ever

ground beef
bok choy, scallions
pinch dried ginger, 1 tablespoon coconut aminos

ground lamb
red bell pepper, green beans, cabbage
Best Stir Fry Sauce Ever

ground lamb
onions, scallions
pinch dried ginger, 1 tablespoon coconut aminos

grilled chicken
snow peas, snap peas, red bell pepper
Best Stir Fry Sauce Ever

grilled chicken
broccoli, red bell pepper
Best Stir Fry Sauce Ever

grilled chicken
celery, green bell pepper
1 tablespoon coconut aminos, cashews

Char Siu (p. 91)
broccoli, cabbage, scallions
1 tablespoon coconut aminos

Central & Eastern EUROPEAN

Top these with fresh minced parsley for a bright flavor that balances the warmer tones of the spices.

ground pork
apples, cabbage
1/2 teaspoon mustard; pinch each of caraway seeds and paprika

ground beef
tomato, mushroom, carrot
pinch each of paprika and marjoram

ground beef or pork
red cabbage, Roasted Spaghetti Squash (p. 123)
Penzeys Tsardust Memories

grilled chicken
Jicama Home Fries (p. 131), apples
pinch each of cinnamon and paprika

FRENCH

To garnish, sprinkle these with fresh minced parsley and a spritz of lemon juice. Serve on a bed of raw baby spinach leaves; the heat from the Hot Plate will wilt the leaves to a tender texture.

ground pork
kale or other greens
dried chives; pinch each of nutmeg, tarragon, cinnamon, and cloves

grilled chicken
carrots, tomato
pinch each of tarragon and chervil

grilled chicken
green beans
1/2 teaspoon Dijon mustard; pinch each of lemon pepper and tarragon

GREEK

These taste great garnished with fresh minced parsley, sliced black olives, and fresh lemon juice. Penzeys Greek Seasoning is a wonderful alternative to the herbs listed below. Serve on a bed of Cauliflower Rice (p. 121); add Mediterranean Mint and Parsley Pesto on the side (p. 53).

ground lamb
tomatoes, eggplant
splash red wine vinegar; pinch each of oregano and marjoram

ground pork or grilled pork chop, sliced very thin
tomatoes, green beans
splash red wine vinegar; pinch each of oregano and marjoram

grilled chicken
tomatoes, zucchini
pinch each of oregano and marjoram

INDIAN

Indian curries taste best when they're slowly simmered, but if you must have the flavors of Indian food **right now**, these will do nicely. You can also use any of these combos with Sri Lankan Curry Sauce (p. 57). Serve on a bed of Basic Cauliflower Rice (p. 121), top with minced cilantro, and enjoy Mint Chutney (p. 53) on the side.

ground lamb
tomatoes, eggplant
2 tablespoons coconut milk
1 teaspoon curry powder

ground lamb
Roasted Spaghetti Squash (p. 123)
2 tablespoons coconut milk
1 teaspoon curry powder

grilled chicken
tomatoes, zucchini
2 tablespoons coconut milk
1 teaspoon curry powder

grilled chicken
cauliflower
2 tablespoons coconut milk
1 teaspoon curry powder

ITALIAN

These are all wonderful on their own or served on a bed of either Roasted Spaghetti Squash (p.123) or Zucchini Noodles Aglio et Olio (p. 133). Just before eating, drizzle the Hot Plate with a 1/2 teaspoon of extra-virgin olive oil.

ground beef
tomatoes, zucchini, black olives
Pizza Seasoning (p. 49)

ground beef
cauliflower, red bell pepper, black olives
Pizza Seasoning (p. 49)

ground beef
tomato, red and green bell peppers
Italian Sausage Seasoning (p. 49)

ground lamb
tomatoes, zucchini, garlic
1/2 teaspoon each of dried rosemary and oregano

grilled chicken
tomatoes, green beans
Basil and Walnut Pesto (p. 53)

grilled chicken
sliced fennel, black olives
pinch of crushed red pepper flakes

grilled chicken
kale
juice of 1/2 lemon

grilled pork chop
tomato, red and green bell peppers
a splash balsamic vinegar, garlic, 1/2 teaspoon dried oregano

MIDDLE EASTERN

Serve on Cauliflower Rice Pilaf (p. 121) with a drizzle of Middle-Eastern Dressing (p. 59). A sprinkle of fresh minced parsley or mint adds zing.

ground lamb
okra
1/4 teaspoon each of cumin and dried mint

ground lamb
any leafy greens
1/4 teaspoon each of cumin and dried mint
pine nuts, juice of 1/2 lemon

MOROCCAN

Serve on Cauliflower rice Pilaf (p. 121 and drizzle with Moroccan Dipping Sauce (p. 55).

ground lamb
tomatoes, zucchini
1/4 teaspoon Ras el Hanout (p. 47)

ground lamb
Roasted Spaghetti Squash (p. 123)
1/4 teaspoon Ras el Hanout (p. 47)

grilled chicken
zucchini, red bell pepper
1/4 teaspoon Ras el Hanout (p. 47)

THAI

Serve on Roasted Spaghetti Squash (p. 123) or Basic Cauliflower Rice (p. 121) and garnish with a squeeze of fresh lime juice.

ground beef
green beans, fresh basil leaves, jalapeño
1 tablespoon each of lime juice and coconut aminos; pinch of red pepper flakes

ground pork
eggplant, fresh basil leaves
1 tablespoon each of lime juice and coconut aminos; pinch of red pepper flakes

grilled chicken
green beans, red bell pepper, mango
Sunshine Sauce (p. 45), cashews

COOL SALADS

SOMETIMES YOU NEED SOMETHING CRISP AND QUICK

ALL-AMERICAN SALAD PLATE

Arrange on a plate: grilled chicken, a hard-boiled egg, raw vegetables, and a serving of Jicama "Potato" Salad (p. 137) or Roni's Creamy Cucumbers (p. 135). Add a ramekin of Ranch or Sweet Mustard Dressing (p. 59) on the side for dipping and a sliced apple or pear for something sweet.

DECONSTRUCTED HAMBURGER SALAD

Toss shredded iceberg lettuce with tomato, onion, and banana pepper rings. Dress with 1 teaspoon each olive oil and vinegar, plus a 1/2 teaspoon of Pizza Seasoning (p. 49). Top with ground beef and a dollop of Olive Oil Mayo (p. 43).

ASIAN CHICKEN SALAD

Toss shredded cabbage, carrots, scallions, and snap peas with diced grilled chicken. Dress with Sunshine Sauce (p. 45), a sprinkle of sliced almonds, and a squeeze of fresh lime juice.

ASIAN TUNA SALAD

Toss baby spinach, slivered red onions, and a few orange sections with a can of drained tuna. Dress with Sunshine Sauce (p. 45) and sprinkle with crushed Sesame-Garlic Nori Chips (p. 129).

ITALIAN ANTIPASTO PLATTER

Arrange on a plate: Mediterranean Tuna Salad (p. 67) or grilled chicken, a hard-boiled egg, black olives and raw vegetables; sprinkle with fresh minced parsley. Add a ramekin of Creamy Italian Dressing (p. 59) on the side for dipping, and a small cluster of grapes for something sweet.

MIDDLE EASTERN MEZE PLATTER

Arrange on a plate: Middle Eastern Tuna Salad (p. 67) or grilled chicken, black olives, raw vegetables, a few little pickles, and a serving of Baba Ghanoush (p. 139); sprinkle with fresh minced parsley and mint. Add a ramekin of Middle-Eastern Dressing (p. 59) on the side for dipping, and a small orange or a few almonds for something sweet.

THAI SALAD PLATTER

Arrange on a plate: grilled chicken or pork chop, snap peas, red bell pepper strips, cucumber slices, carrots, and butter lettuce leaves; sprinkle with fresh minced cilantro. Add a ramekin of Sunshine Sauce (p. 45) on the side for dipping and a small pile of Caramelized Coconut Chips (p. 153) for something sweet.

THE MAGIC OF PARSLEY

A tablespoon of minced parsley leaves is the culinary equivalent of a fresh breeze. When I do my Weekly Cookup, I usually wash a bunch of flat-leaf parsley, pluck the leaves, and store them in a zipper baggie in the fridge, so they're ready to be chopped for garnishes and added to Hot Plates and salads.

CITRUS & SEASONINGS

A spritz of fresh lemon, lime, or orange juice wakes up food. Here are some delicious short cuts to become a citrus master.

LIME:	ORANGE:
CUMIN + CAYENNE	CAYENNE + THYME
	GARLIC + ROSEMARY

LEMON:
GARLIC + OREGANO
CURRY + GINGER
TARRAGON + ONION POWDER
PARSLEY + MINT

FASTEST PACKED LUNCH EVER

If you've got a refrigerator and microwave in your workplace, you don't even need to sauté your Hot Plate before packing it for lunch! I put two cold, steam-sautéed veggies in a portable container, add the right amount of protein, then spoon cold Sri Lankan Curry Sauce (p. 57) on top – or bring Moroccan Dipping Sauce (p. 55), Tahini Dressing (p. 139) or a creamy salad dressing (p. 59) in a separate container. When it's time to eat, I zap the entree container in the microwave and drizzle with the sauce.

In a pinch, I've also used *frozen* veggies; by lunch time, they've defrosted in the fridge and the microwave makes them tender.

NOTES

THAI SALAD PLATTER

Grilled Chicken Thighs

Sunshine Sauce

Caramelized Coconut Chips

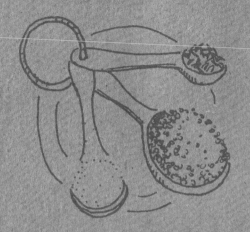

SAUCES
& SEASONINGS

There's no faster, easier, tastier way to add zip and zing to your meals than a pinch of spice blend or a drizzle of luscious dressing.

You can make this super easy by using an immersion blender: Place all ingredients in a wide-mouth jar and blend. Done!

OLIVE OIL MAYO

MAKES 1 ½ cups

PREP	COOK
05 MIN.	N/A

Lemony, light, silky, and luxurious, this mayo makes just about everything better. Indulge with a dollop on grilled meat, transform it into creamy salad dressing in a flash, or stir it into a can of tuna for instant salad. Mix up a batch every week in the blender or food processor to rediscover creamy salads and sauces. (For a video demo of the perfect oil drizzle, visit http://www.theclothesmakethegirl.com/wellfed2)

INGREDIENTS

- 1 large egg
- 2 tablespoons lemon juice
- 1/4 cup plus 1 cup light-tasting olive oil (not extra-virgin!)
- 1/2 teaspoon dry mustard
- 1/2 teaspoon salt

DIRECTIONS

Science! The magic of mayo is that it's an emulsion: The oil and egg plus lemon create a colloid. You don't need to understand all the chemistry, but you do need to bring all of your ingredients to room temperature.

In a blender or food processor, break the egg and add the lemon juice. Put the lid on your appliance and allow the egg and lemon juice to come to room temperature together, at least 30 minutes and up to 2 hours.

When the egg and lemon juice are room temp, add the mustard, salt, and 1/4 cup oil to the canister. Blend on medium until the ingredients are combined. Now the exciting part begins. Your mission is to incorporate the remaining 1 cup oil by pouring very, very slowly. You want the skinniest drizzle you can manage; this takes about 2 to 3 minutes. Breathe. Relax. Sing to yourself.

If you're using a blender, you'll hear the pitch change as the liquid begins to form the emulsion. Eventually, the substance inside the blender will resemble traditional mayonnaise, only far more beautiful. Do not lose your nerve and consider dumping! Continue to drizzle. Slowly.

When all of the oil is incorporated, revel in your triumph and transfer the mayo to a container with a lid. Mark a calendar with your egg expiration date – that's when your mayo expires, too.

NOTES

The blender version is fluffier and thicker; the food processor version is thinner, but still creamy. Both versions will get thicker as they chill in the fridge. If you suffer a mayo "fail," don't despair! It can be used for salad dressing and also firms up a bit when cooled.

YOU KNOW HOW YOU COULD DO THAT?

- *Use cider vinegar instead of lemon juice for a new twist.*
- *Stir in a few chopped, pickled jalapeños for a kick of heat.*

TASTY IDEAS

CREAMY SALAD DRESSINGS, P. 59
TUNA SALADS, P. 67
JICAMA "POTATO" SALAD, P. 137
CUCUMBER SALADS, P. 135

Make a quick version of satay: grill thin slices of steak, chicken, or pork on bamboo skewers, then dip in Sunshine Sauce.

SUNSHINE SAUCE

MAKES 2/3 cup

PREP	COOK
05 MIN.	N/A

It didn't seem like a big deal to me to give up peanuts until I remembered the decadent deliciousness that is peanut sauce. Veggies dipped in peanut sauce. Grilled chicken satay dipped in peanut sauce. Shredded beef wrapped in a butter lettuce leaf with diced red onion and drizzled with... peanut sauce. You get the idea. Then Sunbutter entered my life with its creamy, nutty-flavored goodness, and I got creative.

INGREDIENTS

1/4 cup sunflower seed butter (no sugar added)

2 tablespoons lime juice

1 tablespoon coconut aminos

1/2 teaspoon rice vinegar

1/2 teaspoon crushed red pepper flakes

1/4 teaspoon powdered ginger

dash ground cayenne pepper (optional)

1 clove garlic, minced (about 1 teaspoon)

1/4 cup coconut milk

This sauce never met a raw veggie it didn't like.

DIRECTIONS

Place all the ingredients except the coconut milk in the bowl of a food processor and whirl until well blended.

Scrape down the sides of the bowl with a rubber scraper, then add the coconut milk. Process until it's blended and smooth. Store covered in the fridge.

YOU KNOW HOW YOU COULD DO THAT?

Try almond butter in place of the sunflower seed butter.

TASTY IDEAS
HOT PLATES, P. 35
PAD THAI, P. 63

NOTES
I like Sunbutter brand sunflower seed butter. Be sure to get the sugar-free, organic variety; the only ingredient is organic sunflower seeds.

My first tattoo was inspired by traditional Moroccan henna. It's an intricate design that wraps around my right wrist and ends in a hand of Fatima to ward off the evil eye.

MAKES 1/4 cup

PREP	COOK
05 MIN.	N/A

Ras el Hanout (sounds like rahss el HA-nooT) originated in North Africa thousands of years ago and can include up to 100 individual spices. Each vendor in the market declares his blend to be the best and holds his recipe as a closely-guarded secret. Some people believe the seductive ingredients in Ras el Hanout produce an aphrodisiac. At the very least, any food you season with this exotic blend should inspire diners to kiss the cook.

INGREDIENTS

2 teaspoons salt

2 teaspoons ground cumin

2 teaspoons powdered ginger

2 teaspoons ground black pepper

1 1/2 teaspoons ground cinnamon

1 teaspoon ground coriander

1 teaspoon ground cayenne pepper

1 teaspoon ground allspice

1/2 teaspoon ground cloves

1/4 teaspoon ground nutmeg

DIRECTIONS

Measure all of the spices into a medium bowl and mix with a fork until combined. Close your eyes, take a deep inhale through your nose, and imagine a market in Morocco.

Transfer the spice blend to an airtight container and apply liberally to your food whenever you need a quick getaway to an exotic land.

YOU KNOW HOW YOU COULD DO THAT?

Play around with the quantities of each spice to create your own unique blend, but remember, the goal is a nuanced flavor in which no single spice dominates.

NOTES

Mix 1-2 teaspoons per pound into ground beef or lamb for burgers or meatballs. You can also use it as a rub on steaks, chops, or chicken parts.

TASTY IDEAS

HOT PLATES, P. 35
CREAMY SPICE MARKET KALE, P. 111
VELVETY BUTTERNUT SQUASH, P. 119
CARAMELIZED COCONUT CHIPS, P. 153

MAKES 1/3 cup

PREP	COOK
05 MIN.	N/A

Sausage shouldn't be complicated: It's essentially meat made magical with spices. But too many store-bought brands include sugar and other mystery ingredients. This sugar-free blend works well with ground pork, beef, turkey, and chicken and produces flavorful, worry-free sausage flavor that guarantees you won't need to rely on store bought.

INGREDIENTS

4 teaspoons dried parsley

1 tablespoon dried Italian herbs (I like Penzeys.)

4 teaspoons salt

2 teaspoons ground black pepper

2 teaspoons coarse (granulated) garlic powder

2 teaspoons paprika

1 teaspoon crushed red pepper flakes

1 1/2 teaspoons fennel seed (optional)

DIRECTIONS

In a **medium bowl**, crush the dried parsley and Italian herbs with your fingers or a fork to release their flavor. Add the salt, black pepper, garlic powder, paprika, red pepper flakes, and fennel seed. Mix with a fork and transfer to an airtight container for storage.

TASTY IDEAS

HOT PLATES, P. 35
MEATZA PIE, P. 77
SCOTCH EGGS, P. 83
ITALIAN SAUSAGE AND
    EGGPLANT STRATA, P. 101

YOU KNOW HOW YOU COULD DO THAT?

Same directions, different ingredients.

PIZZA SEASONING

4 teaspoons dried oregano leaves

4 teaspoons dried basil leaves

4 teaspoons dried parsley leaves

1 teaspoon salt

2 teaspoons coarse (granulated) garlic powder

1 teaspoon onion salt (I like Savory Spice Shop's Ornate Onion Salt.)

1/2 teaspoon crushed red pepper flakes

The takeout taste without the pizza hangover.

NOTES

Use 1-2 tablespoons of Italian Sausage Seasoning per 1 pound of ground meat for optimal flavoring. If you want your sausage smokin' hot, increase the paprika and red pepper by about half.

If you'd like to thicken the sauce a bit, stir 1/2 tablespoon arrowroot powder into the sauce with a fork before adding the sauce to the pan.

MAKES 1/3 cup

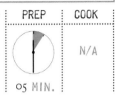

Enough for 1/2 pound of protein and 4 cups veggies

PREP	COOK
05 MIN.	N/A

When I was a small-town kid, my parents would sometimes take my brother and me to a Chinese restaurant in the next town over. There were lush potted palms and a koi pond with a bridge in the middle of the restaurant. The big round table ("our table") had a Lazy Susan in the center of it for sharing dishes. The unfamiliar tastes were irresistible, and I still relish the way a particular flavor can send me on an adventure. Five-spice powder is a crucial ingredient in this sauce and instantly transports local ingredients to an exotic place.

INGREDIENTS

- 1/2 teaspoon rice vinegar
- 1 clove garlic, minced (about 1 teaspoon)
- 2 teaspoons Chinese five-spice powder
- 1/2 teaspoon crushed red pepper flakes
- 2 tablespoons fresh orange juice
- 3 tablespoons coconut aminos

Five-spice powder is sweet, sour, bitter, pungent, and salty.

DIRECTIONS

In a small bowl, mix the vinegar, garlic, five-spice powder, and red pepper flakes with a fork to form a smooth paste. Stirring continuously with the fork, pour in the orange juice, then add the coconut aminos.

YOU KNOW HOW YOU COULD DO THAT?

Substitute other fruit juices for the orange juice: lime, lemon, pomegranate, pineapple.

The way a vegetable is cut affects how quickly it cooks, its texture, and its mouth-feel. Try to cut all your veggies for a stir fry into approximately even-sized pieces so they cook uniformly. Try 1-inch chunks, matchsticks, or thin slices. Change the shape, change your dish.

TASTY IDEAS HOT PLATES, P. 35

NOTES

Use right away in a stir fry or store in a container with a lid in the refrigerator for up to five days.

I like to use walnuts instead of pine nuts in basil pesto because they add a creamy texture that makes up for the absence of cheese. To make the walnuts especially tender, cover them with boiling water and soak for 30-60 minutes before pureeing.

BASIL AND WALNUT PESTO

MAKES 1 cup

	PREP	COOK
	05 MIN.	N/A

If sunshine had a smell, it would be the aroma of basil. Making a batch of homemade pesto can feel like a quick jaunt to a sunny Mediterranean coast. I include a small amount of parsley in this basil pesto to sweeten the leaves a bit in the absence of Parmesan.

INGREDIENTS

- 2 cups fresh basil leaves, packed
- 1/2 cup fresh parsley leaves, packed
- 1/3 cup extra-virgin olive oil
- 1/3 cup walnuts
- 3 cloves garlic, minced (about 1 tablespoon)
- 1/2 teaspoon salt
- 1/8 teaspoon ground black pepper

DIRECTIONS

Puree all ingredients in a blender or food processor to desired consistency. Allow the flavors to meld for about 30 minutes before eating and store in an airtight container in the refrigerator.

TASTY IDEAS

DOLLOP ON GRILLED MEAT, FISH, OR SEAFOOD — OR MIX INTO A CAN OF TUNA FOR A LIGHT TWIST ON TUNA SALAD.

TOSS WITH HOT, COOKED VEGETABLES: SUMMER SQUASH, BROCCOLI, CAULIFLOWER, BABY SPINACH, SPAGHETTI SQUASH, OR DICED TOMATOES.

STIR A SPOONFUL INTO HOT VEGETABLE SOUP OR PLAIN BROTH FOR A CUP OF WARM LOVE.

USE AS A QUICK MARINADE FOR BLACK AND GREEN OLIVES.

YOU KNOW HOW YOU COULD DO THAT?

Same directions, different ingredients.

MEDITERRANEAN PARSLEY-MINT PESTO
1 bunch fresh mint leaves (about 2 cups)
1 cup fresh parsley leaves
juice of half a lemon (about 2 tablespoons)
1/4 cup extra-virgin olive oil
1 clove garlic, minced (about 1 teaspoon)
1/2 teaspoon salt
pinch of crushed red pepper flakes

MINT CHUTNEY
1 bunch fresh mint leaves (about 2 cups)
1/2 fresh jalapeño
1/4 cup fresh parsley leaves
1/4 medium onion, roughly chopped
2 teaspoons lime zest
1 tablespoon fresh lime juice
1/4 teaspoon dried ginger or 1 teaspoon minced fresh
1/4 teaspoon salt

NOTES

Basil pesto turns bitter when it's cooked, so mix pesto into warm foods off the heat to protect the tender aromatics. All types of pesto taste fresh for three to four days.

This sauce is the ideal accessory for unadorned ingredients. Drizzle on a salad of cucumbers, tomatoes, avocado, and onions, steamed green veggies, or any cooked meats.

MAKES ½ cup

PREP	COOK
05 MIN.	N/A

I've yet to encounter a vegetable or grilled meat that wasn't improved by a little drizzle of olive oil and herbs. These two sauces come from opposite sides of the planet but share one lovely characteristic: They make already good food even better. And they both provide a dose of healthy oils. It's an international win-win.

INGREDIENTS

juice of 2 lemons (about 1/4 cup)

1 clove garlic, minced (about 1 teaspoon)

1/2 teaspoon ground cumin

1/4 teaspoon paprika (sweet, hot, or smoked)

pinch ground cayenne pepper

1/2 teaspoon salt

1/4 teaspoon ground black pepper

1/3 cup extra-virgin olive oil

1/2 cup fresh cilantro leaves, minced (about 2 tablespoons)

1/2 cup fresh parsley leaves, minced (about 2 tablespoons)

DIRECTIONS

In a small bowl, whisk together the lemon juice, garlic, cumin, paprika, cayenne, and salt and pepper. Inhale and rejoice that you have a nose.

Gradually whisk in the oil, then stir in the fresh cilantro and parsley.

TASTY IDEAS

HOT PLATES, P. 35
THE BEST CHICKEN YOU WILL EVER EAT, P. 69
SALMON A L'AFRIQUE DU NORD, P. 103

YOU KNOW HOW YOU COULD DO THAT?

Same directions, different ingredients.

CHIMICHURRI SAUCE
2 tablespoons red wine vinegar
4 cloves garlic, minced (about 4 teaspoons)
1 teaspoon salt
1/4 teaspoon ground black pepper
1/2 teaspoon crushed red pepper flakes
1/2 cup extra-virgin olive oil
1 cup firmly packed fresh parsley leaves, minced (about 1/4 cup)
2 tablespoons fresh oregano leaves (or 2 teaspoons dried oregano)

NOTES

These sauces taste best served at room temperature, but should be refrigerated if you're not going to eat them within the hour. They can be kept for two or three days without diminishing their dazzling flavor.

I'm a child of the '80s, and Duran Duran remains one of my favorite bands. Their videos for "Hungry Like The Wolf" and "Save a Prayer" were shot in Sri Lanka against the backdrop of lush jungles, idyllic beaches with wandering elephants, and a marketplace full of intrigue.

SRI LANKAN CURRY SAUCE

SERVES 4 to 6

PREP 05 MIN.

COOK 20 MIN.

I'm a sucker for anything leopard print and any recipe that includes coconut, which sort of explains how this recipe came to be. Sri Lanka is home to the distinctively-spotted Sri Lankan leopard, as well as a traditional dish called "sambol," a paste made of ground coconut, chiles, and lime juice. Sri Lankans don't usually follow strict recipes, so every cook's curry has a unique flavor, just as every leopard's spots are one of a kind. This sauce is slow-simmered on its own, so it can be mixed with any cooked protein and veggies at mealtime for curry in a hurry.

INGREDIENTS

2 medium jalapeño peppers, seeds and ribs removed

1/4 cup unsweetened shredded coconut

2 teaspoons ground coriander

1 teaspoon cinnamon

1 1/2 teaspoons ground cumin

1/2 teaspoon powdered ginger

3/4 teaspoon salt

2 cloves garlic, roughly chopped (about 2 teaspoons)

1/4 cup water

1/2 cup + 1/4 cup coconut milk

1 tablespoon coconut oil

3 medium carrots, grated (about 2 cups)

2 cans (14.5 ounces) diced tomatoes

NOTES

Amp up the heat by using the seeds and ribs when you prep the jalapeños, or turn it down by reducing the number of peppers.

DIRECTIONS

In a food processor, combine the jalapeños, coconut, coriander, cinnamon, cumin, ginger, salt, garlic, and water. Process until it forms a smooth paste, remove to a medium-sized bowl, and stir in 1/2 cup coconut milk with a wooden spoon.

Heat a large non-stick skillet over medium-high, about 3 minutes. Add the coconut oil and allow it to melt. Add the carrots and sauté, stirring with a wooden spoon, until they're tender, about 3 minutes. Add the tomatoes along with their juice. Bring to a boil, then reduce heat to simmer, stirring occasionally and crushing the tomato chunks with the back of the spoon. Cook 7-10 minutes uncovered until the sauce thickens and the vegetables are soft.

Pour in the spice paste, mix well, and add the 1/4 cup coconut milk. Stir to combine, then remove from heat. Use immediately on a Hot Plate (p. 35) or store in a covered container in the refrigerator.

YOU KNOW HOW YOU COULD DO THAT?

This sauce can be customized with any or all of the following:

MINCED CILANTRO
FRESH LIME JUICE
FINELY CHOPPED ALMONDS, CASHEWS, OR MACADAMIAS
THINLY-SLICED SCALLIONS
A SPOONFUL OF SUGAR-FREE SUNFLOWER SEED BUTTER

TASTY IDEAS

HOT PLATES, P. 35

Change the flavor in the Italian dressing by switching up the vinegars. I like pomegranate balsamic, but other infused vinegars are lovely, too.

TASTY IDEAS

- DRIZZLE OVER A FRESHLY-GRILLED BURGER, STEAK, OR CHICKEN.
- USE AS A DIP FOR RED PEPPER STRIPS, CUCUMBER SLICES, TOMATO WEDGES, AND MATCHSTICKS OF JICAMA.
- STIR INTO TUNA, EGG, OR SHRIMP SALAD INSTEAD OF PLAIN MAYO.
- PLACE ON A SPOON. EAT. (I'M ONLY HALFWAY KIDDING.)

CREAMY ITALIAN DRESSING

MAKES 2 to 4

PREP	COOK
05 MIN.	N/A

I was never happy when I found a sandwich in my packed lunch. But I always loved salads, especially with a major dose of creamy Italian dressing. When I was in grade school, my mom would put my lunchtime salad in a Tupperware, then pour just the right amount of bottled creamy Italian dressing in a plastic baggie. All I had to do was cut the corner off the bag and squeeze out the dressing. We grownups mostly toss salad with EVOO and vinegar, but thanks to my homemade mayo, creamy Italian is back on the menu.

INGREDIENTS

1/2 teaspoon dried Italian herb blend or dried oregano

1/4 cup Olive Oil Mayo (p. 43)

1/2 clove garlic, minced (about 1/2 teaspoon)

2 tablespoons vinegar: balsamic, wine, or cider

salt and black pepper, to taste

DIRECTIONS

In a small bowl, crush the dried herbs with your fingers, then add mayo and garlic. Blend well with a fork.

Drizzle in the vinegar, mixing with the fork, then taste and season with salt and pepper. If your dressing is too thick, add either vinegar or water – a 1/4 teaspoon at a time – until it's the right consistency. Keep in mind that it will thin slightly as you toss it with your salad ingredients.

YOU KNOW HOW YOU COULD DO THAT?

Same directions, different ingredients.

SOUTHWEST CUMIN-LIME DRESSING

1/4 cup Olive Oil Mayo (p. 43)
1/2 clove garlic, minced (about 1/2 teaspoon)
1/4 teaspoon ground cumin
a few jalapeño rings, finely minced (optional)
1 tablespoon lime juice
salt and black pepper, to taste

RANCH DRESSING

1/4 cup Olive Oil Mayo (p. 43)
1/2 clove garlic, minced (about 1/2 teaspoon)
1/8 teaspoon paprika
2 tablespoons fresh parsley leaves, minced (about 1 tablespoon)
2 teaspoons dried chives
1/2 teaspoon lemon juice
salt and black pepper, to taste

MIDDLE EASTERN DRESSING

1/2 teaspoon dried mint
1/4 cup Olive Oil Mayo (p. 43)
2 tablespoons fresh parsley leaves, minced (about 1 tablespoon)
1/2 teaspoon za'atar
1/2 teaspoon crushed red pepper flakes or Aleppo pepper
1/2 clove garlic, minced (about 1/2 teaspoon)
1 tablespoon lemon juice
salt and black pepper, to taste

SWEET MUSTARD DRESSING

1/4 cup Olive Oil Mayo
1/2 teaspoon dried mustard
1/2 clove garlic, minced (about 1/2 teaspoon)
2 teaspoons unsweetened applesauce
1 teaspoon cider vinegar
salt and black pepper, to taste

I've given instructions for a smallish quantity so it's made "to order." I don't recommend that you make a big batch in advance; the texture will suffer. It takes so little time to blend, make it fresh. Your tastebuds will thank you.

PROTEIN

From slow-simmered stews to grilled meats and seafood to comforting casseroles, these recipes have your protein needs covered. Most of them include veggies, too, but their primary *raison d'être* is the protein punch!

Thai food is usually served with a variety of condiments. Arrange small bowls of garnishes and let your dining companions customize their plates the way they like 'em.

PAD THAI SLINKY, SILKY NOODLES FROM SIAM

SERVES 2

PREP	COOK
15 MIN.	05 MIN.

Sometimes you just want a pile of something spicy-creamy-comforting like Pad Thai. But the original dish uses rice noodles (fail), soy sauce (fail), peanuts (fail), and sugar (fail) to create the delicate Thai balance of sour, sweet, and salty. This version is Pad Thai you can feel good about eating, emotionally and physically. There's a touch of rice vinegar in the Sunshine Sauce for sourness, snap peas for sweetness, and coconut aminos for saltiness. The ingredients combine to create a dish with just the right feeling on your tongue: creamy, rich, and luxurious.

INGREDIENTS

- 1 batch Sunshine Sauce (p. 45)
- 2 large eggs
- 2 teaspoons coconut aminos
- 2 teaspoons plus 1 teaspoon coconut oil
- 1/2 medium onion, thinly sliced (about 1/2 cup)
- 1 cup snap peas, thinly sliced lengthwise
- 2 cups Roasted Spaghetti Squash (p. 123)
- 6-8 ounces Grilled Chicken Thighs, diced (p. 29)

OPTIONAL GARNISHES:

CHOPPED TOASTED CASHEWS OR ALMONDS

SUNFLOWER SEEDS

SLICED SCALLIONS

MINCED CILANTRO

A SQUEEZE OF LIME JUICE

DIRECTIONS

Crack the eggs into a small bowl, and use a fork to scramble them with the coconut aminos. Heat a large skillet over medium-high heat, about 3 minutes. Add 2 teaspoons coconut oil to the skillet, and when it's melted, pour in the eggs and let them spread like a pancake. Reduce the heat to medium and cover with a lid, letting the eggs cook until they're set and beginning to brown on the bottom, about 3-4 minutes. Flip and lightly brown the other side. Remove the eggs from the pan and cut into strips with a sharp knife.

Using the same pan, increase heat to medium-high and add 1 teaspoon coconut oil to the pan. Sauté the onion and snap peas, stirring with a wooden spoon, until they're crisp-tender, about 2 minutes. Add the spaghetti squash, chicken, and cooked egg to the pan and, stirring with a wooden spoon, cook until heated through, about 3 minutes.

Add the Sunshine Sauce to the pan and stir-fry until everything is well-blended and hot. Divide among two plates, sprinkle with garnishes, and dig in.

YOU KNOW HOW YOU COULD DO THAT?

- *Replace grilled chicken with Ginger-Lime Grilled Shrimp (p. 75) or Char Siu (p. 91).*
- *Swap Zucchini Noodles Aglio et Olio (p. 133) for spaghetti squash.*
- *Use chopped steam-sautéed broccoli or cabbage in place of snap peas (p. 33).*

NOTES

Serve this with thin slices of fresh cucumber and bell pepper rings for a cool, crisp contrast to the creamy noodles.

Like all great stews, this one improves with age. Just make some fresh gremolata to sprinkle on the leftovers for maximum effect.

TASTES GREAT WITH

MASHED CAULIFLOWER, P. 113
BASIC CAULIFLOWER RICE, P. 121
ROASTED SPAGHETTI SQUASH, P. 123

SERVES 6 to 10

PREP
30 MIN.

COOK
90 MIN.

Stews are lovely because while they simmer, I forget that I'm the one who made them. When it's time to sit down and eat, I feel as if someone else cooked for me. What a treat! In this flavorful stew, the cinnamon and herbs create a mellow, earthy gravy that's a foil for the bright, tart taste of the orange gremolata on top. It's sophisticated comfort food.

INGREDIENTS

STEW:

2-3 pounds beef stew meat, cut into 1-inch cubes

salt and black pepper, to taste

3 tablespoons coconut oil

1 medium carrot, peeled and finely chopped (about 1/4 cup)

1 medium onion, diced (about 1 cup)

1 medium celery stalk, finely chopped (about 1/4 cup)

2 cloves garlic, minced (about 2 teaspoons)

2 tablespoons tomato paste

1/2 cup beef broth

2 tablespoons balsamic vinegar

3-5 cups water

2 teaspoons salt

1 teaspoon ground black pepper

2 bay leaves

1 sprig fresh rosemary
   (or 1/2 teaspoon dried)

1 sprig fresh thyme
   (or 1/2 teaspoon dried)

1 sprig fresh sage
   (or 1/2 teaspoon dried)

2 cinnamon sticks

extra-virgin olive oil,
   for garnish (optional)

ORANGE GREMOLATA:

1/2 cup fresh parsley leaves, finely
   minced (about 2 tablespoons)

zest from 1 orange
   (about 2 tablespoons)

leaves from 1 sprig fresh thyme
   (1/2 teaspoon dried)

2 cloves garlic, minced
   (about 2 teaspoons)

1/2 teaspoon rose water (optional)

DIRECTIONS

Sprinkle the beef generously with salt and pepper. In a large pot or Dutch oven, heat the coconut oil over medium-high heat, then add the meat in batches and sear on all sides. It's important that you don't crowd the pan. The meat needs air around it to achieve a crisp brown crust. With tongs or a slotted spoon, remove the browned pieces to a bowl to catch their juice. Repeat with the remaining cubes.

In the same pot, sauté the chopped carrot, onion, celery, and garlic for about 2 minutes, stirring with a wooden spoon. Add the tomato paste and stir for about 1 minute.

Deglaze the pan. Which is just a cook's way to say: Add the broth and vinegar, then stir with passion, scraping up all the wonderful brown bits at the bottom of the pan. Keep stirring until the mixture starts to thicken.

Put the meat and its drippings back into the pot. Add 3 cups water, 2 teaspoons salt, a healthy dose of pepper, the bay leaves, rosemary, thyme, sage, and cinnamon sticks.

Bring to a boil, then reduce the heat and simmer with the pot only partially covered for about 90 minutes. This is not a soupy stew, but if the stew starts to dry out, add more water, about a 1/2 cup at a time. Simmer until the meat is fall-apart tender and the liquid in the pan has been reduced to gravy-like status.

During the last 15 minutes of stew cooking time, make the gremolata. In a small bowl, mix the parsley, orange zest, thyme, garlic, and rose water.

Remove the cinnamon sticks and herb stems from the stew pot. Ladle the stew into deep bowls and top with a few pinches of orange gremolata. Bonus points if you also add a light drizzle of olive oil.

Eat the orange gremolata immediately to enjoy the full effects of the aromatic orange oils. It will keep in the refrigerator for a few days, but it's best when it's fresh.

Waldorf salad appeared in a cookbook in 1928 and was so popular, it was featured in Cole Porter's "You're the Top" from the musical *Anything Goes*.

You're the top! You're a Waldorf salad.
You're the top! You're a Berlin ballad.
You're the boats that glide on the sleepy Zuider Zee,
You're an old Dutch master, You're Lady Astor,
You're broccoli!

WALDORF TUNA SALAD

SERVES 2

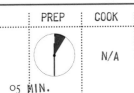

PREP ○5 MIN. | COOK N/A

When we made Waldorf Salad in sixth-grade home ec, I declined to eat it. To my 8-year-old mind, the original Waldorf salad – created at the Waldorf Astoria Hotel – sounded both gross (apples and mayo?!) and romantic (a glittery hotel in Manhattan!). But now, I appreciate its elegance, its short preparation time, and the contrast of crisp apples and tangy mayo.

INGREDIENTS

1 small apple, diced (about 1 cup)

2-3 scallions, dark green tops only, thinly sliced (about 1/4 cup)

4 pecan halves, coarsely chopped (about 2 tablespoons)

1/4 cup fresh parsley leaves, minced (about 1 tablespoon)

2 cans (5 ounce) tuna

1/2 teaspoon mustard powder

3-4 tablespoons Olive Oil Mayo (p. 43)

salt and black pepper, to taste

DIRECTIONS

Place apple, scallion tops, nuts, and parsley in a medium-sized bowl and mix with a fork.

Drain the liquid from the tuna and add the tuna to the bowl. Mash with a fork to break it up until no big chunks remain.

Add the mustard and mayo to the bowl and mix with a rubber spatula until blended. Try a bite, then add salt and pepper to adjust the seasonings. If you can stand it, let the tuna salad sit for 15 minutes so the flavors meld.

TASTY IDEAS

ROLL THE TUNA SALAD IN BUTTER LETTUCE LEAVES TO MAKE WRAPS, OR SPOON INTO RED PEPPER HALVES OR CUCUMBER BOATS. INSTANT PARTY FOOD! YOU MIGHT ALSO TRY SWAPPING STEAMED SHRIMP FOR THE TUNA.

YOU KNOW HOW YOU COULD DO THAT?

Same directions, different ingredients.

MEDITERRANEAN TUNA SALAD
10 black olives, pitted and sliced
2-3 banana peppers, sliced into rings
10 fresh mint leaves, minced (about 1 tablespoon) or 1/4 teaspoon dried mint leaves
1/4 cup fresh parsley leaves, minced (about 1 tablespoon)
1 teaspoon lemon juice
salt and black pepper, to taste

MIDDLE EASTERN TUNA SALAD
1/4 cup fresh parsley leaves, minced (about 1 tablespoon)
1/4 teaspoon za'atar
1/4 teaspoon crushed red pepper flakes or Aleppo pepper
1/4 teaspoon dried mint leaves
1/4 teaspoon ground cumin
1 teaspoon lemon juice
salt and black pepper, to taste

TEX-MEX TUNA SALAD
1/4 cup fresh cilantro leaves, minced (about 1 tablespoon)
1/4 cup avocado, diced (about 1/2 small avocado)
1/4 cup tomato, diced (about 1/2 small tomato)
1/4 teaspoon chili powder
1/8 teaspoon ground cumin
1 teaspoon lime juice
salt and black pepper, to taste

No grill? Apply the Secrets as directed, but bake chicken in a 400 F oven for 15-20 minutes instead of grilling.

Leftovers don't feel like leftovers when they're sliced and piled atop a salad of butter lettuce, very thin slices of cucumber, and slivered red onion, then dressed with Moroccan Dipping Sauce (p. 55).

THE BEST CHICKEN YOU WILL EVER EAT
INSPIRED BY COOK'S ILLUSTRATED & AN ESSAY BY MICHAEL POLLAN

SERVES 6 to 12

BRINING	PREP	COOK
x2		
2 HRS.	10 MIN.	08 MIN.

The grill is not always kind to our lean, reliable friend, the skinless, boneless breast. But this recipe unlocks the secrets of juicy, flavorful meat with minimal work. Infused with zing from a relatively quick brining and coated in a fragrant blend of spices, this chicken gets a sexy finish with a drizzle of Moroccan Dipping Sauce.

INGREDIENTS

BRINING:

2 garlic cloves, whole

8 cups water

3 tablespoons salt

1/2 tablespoon coconut aminos

1 bay leaf

1 teaspoon whole coriander seeds

1 teaspoon whole cumin seeds

1 teaspoon whole black peppercorns

2-3 pounds boneless,
skinless chicken breasts

SPICE BLEND:

1 tablespoon ground cumin

1 tablespoon curry powder

1 tablespoon chili powder

1/2 tablespoon ground allspice

1/2 teaspoon ground cinnamon

3/4 teaspoon ground black pepper

2 tablespoons coconut oil

Thanks for introducing me to brining. Quite possibly the moistest boneless, skinless, chicken breast I've ever had. I have always heard about brining but thought it was super complicated. Easy.

—Anna, a blog reader

DIRECTIONS

SECRET #1: BRINING

You will think this step is not necessary. You will, perhaps, find it too fussy. Ignore those feelings, and put the chicken in the salty spa. Trust.

Place the garlic cloves on a cutting board and place the flat side of a knife on top of them. With your fist, lightly strike the knife to crack the cloves, then remove and discard the peel.

Place a 1-gallon zipper storage bag inside a large bowl so it's standing up. Pour the water into the bag, then add the garlic, salt, coconut aminos, bay leaf, coriander seeds, cumin seeds, and peppercorns. Stir with your hand to dissolve the salt, then add the chicken to the bag. This will look a bit unappetizing; avert your eyes.

Seal the bag and place the bowl in the refrigerator for 2 hours, then rinse the chicken well, and set it in a colander to dry while you move on to Secret #2. If you want, you can stop here, wrap and refrigerate the chicken, then grill it another day; it will survive in the fridge for 2-3 days.

SECRET #2: SPICE BLEND

Preheat a gas grill on high heat, with the lid closed, about 10 minutes.

Place all the spice blend ingredients except the coconut oil in a small bowl and mix with a fork. Put the coconut oil in a microwave-safe dish and heat until melted, about 15 seconds. Pour the melted oil into the spice blend and combine with a fork.

Coat the chicken pieces with the mixture. You can either massage it on lovingly by hand or toss it in a bowl with enthusiasm until the chicken is coated.

Place the chicken smooth side down on the preheated grill, close the lid, and cook for 4 minutes. Flip the chicken, cook for an additional 3-4 minutes with the lid closed, until the chicken is browned and cooked through.

NOTE: Any leftover spice blend needs to be discarded. Don't re-use it on vegetables or think you can save it for later. It's once and done when raw chicken is involved.

SECRET #3: DIPPING SAUCE

The Moroccan Dipping Sauce is perhaps the best secret of all; see page 55.

YOU KNOW HOW YOU COULD DO THAT?

This technique and spice blends works wonders on boneless chicken thighs and lean pork chops, too. Increase grill time to about 5 minutes per side.

TASTES GREAT WITH

MIDDLE EASTERN CUCUMBERS, P. 135

BABA GHANOUSH, P. 139

EL MINZAH ORANGE SALAD, P. 143

MOROCCAN MEATBALLS

SERVES 6 to 8

MAKES	PREP	COOK
about 36 meatballs	15 MIN.	60 MIN.

Morocco has long been on my list of must-visit countries. Twisting alleys, markets crowded with vendors, scampering trained monkeys... I need to see it all. The country sits in the northwestern corner of Africa, and the influence of Arab and Moorish invaders can be tasted in traditional Moroccan cuisine. Lucky us! Spices like aromatic cinnamon, cumin, and paprika are prevalent, along with herbs like mint and parsley. These meatballs are seasoned with essential Moroccan spices, then simmered in tomatoes that cloak them in a sauce that tastes like mystery and adventure.

INGREDIENTS

Lamb and beef are both popular in Morocco, so a blend of ground beef and lamb is a good way to roll.

MEATBALLS:

1/2 cup fresh parsley leaves, minced (about 2 tablespoons)

1 tablespoon paprika

2 teaspoons ground cumin

1 teaspoon salt

1/4 teaspoon ground black pepper

2 pounds ground lamb

SAUCE:

1 tablespoon coconut oil

2 medium onions, diced (about 2 cups)

2 garlic cloves, crushed (about 2 teaspoons)

2 teaspoons paprika

2 teaspoons ground cumin

1 teaspoon salt

1/4 teaspoon ground black pepper

2 medium tomatoes, diced (about 2 cups)

1 1/2 cups water

2/3 cup tomato paste

1/2 cup fresh parsley leaves, minced (about 2 tablespoons)

GARNISH:

1/4 cup roasted pistachios, chopped

DIRECTIONS

In a large mixing bowl, combine the parsley, paprika, cumin, salt, and pepper with a fork. With your hands, crumble the lamb into the bowl and knead until all of the ingredients are incorporated.

Moisten your hands with water and shake to remove excess. Measure a level tablespoon of lamb and roll into a ball between your palms. Line up the meatballs on a baking sheet until it's time to put them in the sauce.

Heat the oil in a large, deep skillet or pot. Add the onion and sauté until soft, about 5 minutes. Add the garlic, paprika, cumin, salt, and pepper and stir until fragrant, about 30 seconds. Add the chopped tomatoes to the pan and stir about 1 minute. Add the water, tomato paste, and parsley, mixing to dissolve the tomato paste.

Bring the sauce to a boil, then gently place the meatballs in the skillet, cover, and reduce heat to simmer. Cook 40 minutes covered, then remove the lid and cook an additional 20 minutes, until the sauce has thickened. Sprinkle each serving with a few teaspoons of chopped pistachios.

YOU KNOW HOW YOU COULD DO THAT?

To make it just like a cook would in Marrakesh, carefully break a few eggs on top of the meatballs when they're finished cooking, and let the sauce gently poach the eggs until the yolks are firm.

TASTES GREAT WITH

MASHED CAULIFLOWER, P. 113
CAULIFLOWER RICE PILAF, P. 121
ROASTED SPAGHETTI SQUASH, P. 123
ZUCCHINI NOODLES AGLIO ET OLIO, P. 133

CHOCOLATE CHILI YEAH, THAT'S RIGHT. CHOCOLATE.

SERVES 6 to 8

PREP 20 MIN.

COOK 2-3 HRS.

In sixth-grade English, our class read a story about a Native American tribe in the Southwest. I've forgotten all but one fascinating detail of that story: The family ate meat cooked with chocolate. Thanks to my dad's rule that we must at least try everything once, I ate a lot of weird stuff as a kid – raw lamb in kibbeh, sweetbreads, capers – but this was something I simply couldn't fathom. Chocolate! With meat! Now, I'm a sucker for anything that's sweetly savory, and every time I reach for the cocoa, I smile at the memory of 11-year-old me. This chili is spicy, but not hot. Reminiscent of mole, the flavors are rich, mellow, and deep.

INGREDIENTS

2 tablespoons coconut oil

2 medium onions, diced (about 2 cups)

4 cloves garlic, minced (about 4 teaspoons)

2 pounds ground beef

1 teaspoon dried oregano leaves

2 tablespoons chili powder

2 tablespoons ground cumin

1 1/2 tablespoons unsweetened cocoa

1 teaspoon ground allspice

1 teaspoon salt

1 can (6 ounces) tomato paste

1 can (14.5 ounces) fire-roasted, chopped tomatoes

2 cups beef broth

1 cup water

Simmering is the magic time when the flavors meld and, like most tomato-based, slow-simmer foods, this tastes even better on the second (or third) day.

NOTES

DIRECTIONS

Heat a large, deep pot over medium-high heat, then add the coconut oil. When the oil is melted, add onions, stir with a wooden spoon and cook until they're translucent, about 7 minutes. Add the garlic and as soon as it's fragrant, about 30 seconds, crumble the ground meat into the pan with your hands, mixing with the wooden spoon to combine. Continue to cook the meat, stirring often, until it's no longer pink.

In a small bowl, crush the oregano between your palms to release its flavor, then add the chili powder, cumin, cocoa, allspice, and salt. Combine with a fork, then add to the pot, stirring like you mean it. Add tomato paste and stir until combined, about 2 minutes.

Add the tomatoes with their juice, beef broth, and water to the pot. Stir well. Bring to a boil, then reduce the heat so the chili enjoys a gentle simmer. Simmer uncovered for at least 2 hours. Do not skimp on the simmer!

YOU KNOW HOW YOU COULD DO THAT?

- *Try a meat combo by mixing ground beef with ground turkey, pork, or bison.*
- *Make a double batch and freeze half so you have chili-on-demand.*
- *Top with sliced olives, diced onions, and/or avocado slices.*

TASTY IDEAS

PLACE A GENEROUS HELPING OF ROASTED SPAGHETTI SQUASH (P. 123), MASHED CAULIFLOWER (P. 113), OR A HANDFUL OF RAW BABY SPINACH LEAVES IN THE BOTTOM OF YOUR CHILI BOWL. VEGGIE POWER!

Go tropical! Add cubes of fresh pineapple to the skewers and replace the lime juice with pineapple juice. Bonus points if you sprinkle the skewers with shredded, unsweetened coconut when they come off the grill.

GINGER-LIME GRILLED SHRIMP

SERVES 3 to 4

PREP	MARINATE	COOK
05 MIN.	20 MIN.	06 MIN.

Ridiculously fast and easy to make, these shrimp are packed with a one-two punch of garlic and ginger, followed by a touch of lime that tingles the tongue. The natural sweetness of the shrimp complements the citrus, and the touch of char from the grill is a nice partner for the firm flesh of the seafood.

INGREDIENTS

juice of 1 lime (about 2 tablespoons)

1/4 teaspoon crushed red pepper flakes

3 cloves garlic, minced (about 1 tablespoon)

2 teaspoons freshly-grated ginger (about a 2-inch piece)

1/4 teaspoon salt

1/4 teaspoon ground black pepper

2 tablespoons fresh cilantro leaves, minced (about 1 tablespoon)

1 tablespoon extra-virgin olive oil

1-2 pounds large shrimp

DIRECTIONS

In a small bowl, squeeze the lime to extract the juice, then add the red pepper flakes, garlic, ginger, salt, black pepper, and cilantro. Mix well with a fork, then drizzle in the oil, stirring constantly.

With a small, sharp knife, pierce the shrimp at the head end and carefully cut along the back toward the tail, removing the dark vein. Rinse in running water. Pat dry, then place the shrimp in a medium bowl and mix with the marinade. Cover tightly and refrigerate for 20 minutes.

Preheat the gas grill on high heat with the lid closed, about 10 minutes. Thread the shrimp on skewers, leaving a little room between them so they don't steam. Grill 2-3 minutes per side with the lid closed.

NOTES:

To get maximum juice from your lime, roll it a few times (with purpose!) on the countertop under your palm before cutting. This breaks up the membranes and loosens the juice inside.

YOU KNOW HOW YOU COULD DO THAT?

Try it on scallops or cubes of dense white fish, chicken breast, or pork chops.

TASTES GREAT WITH

CAULIFLOWER RICE PILAF, P. 121

COCONUT-ALMOND GREEN BEANS, P. 125

ZUCCHINI NOODLES AGLIO ET OLIO, P. 133

Make the crust, sauce, and veggies in advance – they hold up great in the fridge or freezer – then assemble anytime you want pizza. Faster than delivery!

MAKES

2 6-inch meatzas

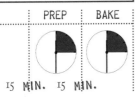

PREP   BAKE

15 MIN.   15 MIN.

My perfect Friday night? Pizza and a movie on the couch. Some might argue it's the cheese that makes a pizza, but I disagree. I think it's the friendly wedge shape of the slices — and that they're meant to be eaten with our hands. Then there's the play of oregano and garlic against the sweetness of the tomato sauce, and the slightly guilty pleasure of just a little grease. So go ahead! Pop in a rental movie, slide a slice of meatza pie onto a paper plate, and snuggle in.

INGREDIENTS

MEAT CRUST:

1 pound ground beef
2 teaspoons Italian Sausage Seasoning
  (p. 49)

SAUCE:

1 teaspoon olive oil
1 clove garlic, minced
  (about 1 teaspoon)
1 teaspoon Pizza Seasoning (p. 49)
3 ounces tomato paste (1/2 can)
1/4 cup water

TOPPINGS:

1/4 cup steam-sautéed broccoli (p. 33)
1/4 cup steam-sautéed bell pepper strips
10 black olives, pitted and sliced
a handful of fresh baby spinach leaves

Instead of individual round pizzas, use a 13x9-inch pan. Cut it into small squares for portable party food.

DIRECTIONS

Preheat the oven to 400F. Mix the ground beef and Italian Sausage Seasoning until combined.

Make the meat crust. Divide the meat in half, roll into a ball, and press evenly into an 8- or 9-inch round pie pan. Cover only the bottom of the pan and smooth the meat with damp hands until it's an even thickness. Repeat with the other piece of "crust." Bake for 10-15 minutes, until the meat is cooked through and the edges are brown. Leaving the oven on, remove the crusts from the oven and allow to cool in the pan.

Make the pizza sauce. Heat a small saucepan over low heat, then add the olive oil, garlic, and Pizza Seasoning, stirring with a wooden spoon until fragrant, about 20 seconds. Add the tomato paste and stir until combined, then stir in the water. Bring to a boil, then simmer uncovered for 5 minutes until thickened. Set aside.

Make your meatza. Cover a large baking sheet with parchment paper or aluminum foil and place the meat crusts on the baking sheet. Spread about 1/4 cup sauce on each meat crust, leaving a 1/2-inch border around the edges. Arrange the vegetables on top, pressing them gently into the sauce. Pop the pizza back into the oven for 10-15 minutes, until hot and browned to your liking.

Bonus! Drizzle each pizza with 1 teaspoon of extra-virgin olive oil when they come out of the oven.

YOU KNOW HOW YOU COULD DO THAT?

Eliminate the Italian Sausage Seasoning from the crust and instead, use salt, black pepper, and 2 cloves of minced garlic to flavor the meat crust. Replace the pizza sauce with the sauces listed below, then add the recommended toppings for a whole new world of flavors.

BEEF CRUST + PIZZA SAUCE + FRESH TOMATO, FRESH BASIL, GARLIC

BEEF CRUST + NO SAUCE + CARAMELIZED ONIONS, FENNEL, GARLIC, BLACK OLIVES

BEEF CRUST + PIZZA SAUCE + MUSHROOMS, PROSCIUTTO

BEEF CRUST + SALSA + BLACK OLIVES, GREEN BELL PEPPER, AVOCADO

BEEF CRUST + PESTO (P. 53) + SUNDRIED TOMATOES, ROASTED RED PEPPER, BLACK OLIVES

BEEF CRUST + PIZZA SAUCE + KALE, BACON, TOMATO

PORK CRUST + SUNSHINE SAUCE (P. 45) + SCALLIONS, CARROTS, RED BELL PEPPER, SESAME SEEDS

PORK CRUST + A LITTLE MUSTARD + CABBAGE, APPLES, CARAWAY SEEDS

LAMB CRUST + BABA GHANOUSH (P. 139) + RAISINS, PINE NUTS, RED BELL PEPPER

LAMB CRUST + TAHINI DRESSING (P. 139) + BABY SPINACH, BLACK OLIVES, TOMATO

LAMB CRUST + NO SAUCE + ZUCCHINI, FRESH TOMATO, DRIED OREGANO

Carne seca *is available in most grocery stores; substitute dried beef or beef jerky in a pinch. But check your ingredient labels! The only ingredients in the package should be beef and spices.*

SERVES 2

PREP	COOK
05 MIN.	10 MIN.

Machacado and eggs is a Mexican dish made from shredded, dried beef (called carne seca)*, eggs, diced onion and tomato, with a touch of jalapeño. This style of dried beef originated near Monterrey, Mexico. As the legend goes, a woman named Tia Lencha was the first to mix the air-cured local beef with eggs. She eventually sold the recipe to a restaurant, and now, the Tia Lencha brand of carne seca is available in grocery stores all over Mexico. This dish is my standard Saturday morning breakfast, and I especially like it after a tough workout. The dried beef has just the right amount of saltiness, and its chewiness is a lovely contrast to the tender scrambled eggs.*

INGREDIENTS

AVOCADO RELISH:

1/2 avocado, cut into 1/2-inch dice (about 1/2 cup)

1/4 cup cilantro leaves, minced (about 1 tablespoon)

1/4 medium red onion, minced (about 2 tablespoons)

2 teaspoons fresh lime juice (about 1/2 a lime)

salt and black pepper, to taste

MACHACADO AND EGGS:

6 large eggs

salt and black pepper, to taste

coconut oil, for sautéing

2 ounces carne seca (a.k.a., machacado) or dried beef

1/4 medium onion, diced (about 1/4 cup)

1 clove garlic, minced (about 1 teaspoon)

1/2 jalapeño, ribs and seeds removed, finely diced (about 1 tablespoon)

1/2 medium tomato, seeded and diced (about 1/2 cup)

1/4 teaspoon chili powder

TASTES GREAT WITH

CHIMICHURRI SAUCE, P. 55
JICAMA HOME FRIES, P. 131

DIRECTIONS

Place all the ingredients for the avocado relish in a small bowl and mix gently with a fork until just combined; you want the avocado to retain its structural integrity. Set aside to allow the flavors to meld while you make the eggs.

Crack the eggs into a medium bowl, sprinkle with salt and pepper, then lightly beat with a fork or whisk. Set aside.

Heat a skillet over medium-high heat and add 1 tablespoon coconut oil. When the pan is hot, add the carne seca, onion, garlic, jalapeño, tomato, and chili powder. Sauté, stirring with a wooden spoon, until the onions are tender and beginning to get nice brown spots, about 7-10 minutes.

Push the vegetables and beef to the side of the pan and add 1 tablespoon coconut oil. Add the scrambled eggs to the pan and push the meat and veggies into the egg. Let it all rest for a bit so the egg begins to set around the other ingredients, then gently stir with a wooden spoon. Continue to gently scramble until cooked to your liking; personal preference should dictate cooking time. Taste a bite, then add salt and pepper.

NOTES

Nori is one-third protein and is packed with iodine, carotene, and vitamins A, B, and C, along with lots of calcium and iron. Make Nori Chips, too! (p. 129)

TASTY IDEAS

SERVE WITH A SLAW MADE FROM SHREDDED CABBAGE, A DASH OF SESAME OIL, A SPLASH OF RICE VINEGAR, AND A SPRINKLE OF TOASTED SESAME SEEDS.

SERVES 1 to 2

PREP	COOK
10 MIN.	N/A

Confession: My favorite kind of sushi is the California roll. I know it doesn't have the elegance of sashimi, but here's the thing: it's got the flavor and texture mélange (mélange!) of cool, sweet seafood with creamy avocado, salty coconut aminos, and the bite-you-back of wasabi. There's also plenty to love in the nutrition department. Seafood and fish are excellent protein sources, and avocado is a first-rate source of monounsaturated fat (a.k.a., the good kind). Plus, sushi is fun to eat. You like fun, right?

I've included two versions to get you started: Mango-Shrimp Roll and Avocado-Salmon Roll.

INGREDIENTS

1 medium avocado

1/2 medium mango

1 medium red bell pepper

2-3 scallions, green tops only

1 medium cucumber

1/4 jicama (about 1/4 pound)

4 ounces shrimp, steamed and chilled
(I used wild, cold-water salad shrimp)

4 ounces smoked salmon

4 sheets nori

wasabi powder, coconut aminos (optional)

DIRECTIONS

PREP YOUR INGREDIENTS

Avocado: Cut in half and remove the pit. Use a spoon to remove the fruit from the skin and slice the avocado lengthwise into thin slivers.

Mango: Peel the mango, remove the pit, and cut half of it into strips lengthwise. Reserve the other half for dessert!

Red pepper: Cut in half, remove stem and ribs, then slice into very thin strips lengthwise.

Scallions: Cut in half to separate the dark green tops from the white, then cut the dark green tops into strips lengthwise.

Cucumber: Peel, cut in half lengthwise and remove the seeds with a spoon, then cut into matchsticks.

Jicama: Cut in half, peel, then cut a slice into matchsticks.

Wasabi: If using, mix wasabi with water, following the package instructions, and set aside.

- -

ASSEMBLE

Lay a piece of nori on a rolling mat, shiny side down. With about 1/4 of the avocado, form a single layer of slices on the nori. Leave a naked 1-inch strip on the side closest to you. Use the back of a spoon to spread the avocado across the surface of the nori. It doesn't need to cover it completely – just enough to help seal the roll and soften the nori. Repeat with all 4 nori sheets.

We'll start with Mango-Shrimp. Place half the shrimp on the bare strip of nori closest to you and top them with a few of the scallion greens. Place a parallel stripe of mango on the far-side front of the shrimp, and add a few strips of red pepper on top of the mango.

Time to roll. Starting at the end closest to you, take a deep breath and roll the sushi, using the mat to help you tuck the ingredients into the roll. When you get to the end, give it a gentle squeeze to help the avocado do its job. Repeat with the remaining shrimp and another sheet of nori.

Now the Avocado-Salmon. Place half the salmon on the bare strip of nori closest to you and top it with a few of the scallion greens. Place a parallel strip of jicama in front of the salmon, and add a few matchsticks of cucumber on top of the jicama. Roll, starting with the end closest to you, then repeat with the remaining salmon and remaining sheet of nori.

Slice and serve. Run a sharp knife under water and shake to remove the excess. Slice the roll crosswise into rounds about 1-inch thick and arrange on a plate, along with the remaining vegetables to eat on the side. If you're dipping, add some coconut aminos to your wasabi and dig in.

Don't have a sushi mat? Don't fret! Just follow the instructions and use a piece of construction paper in place of the bamboo rolling mat.

YOU KNOW HOW YOU COULD DO THAT?

- *Add cooked and cooled scrambled egg, cut into strips.*
- *Replace shrimp with crab or lobster.*
- *Mix seafood with a little Olive Oil Mayo (p. 43) and wasabi powder.*

Do yourself a favor: read Jane Eyre, or at least watch the Masterpiece Theater adaptation on DVD. You might also want to get lost in British mysteries by Dick Francis or Elizabeth George.

SCOTCH EGGS PERFECT FOR SUPPER OR TEA

SERVES 4 to 8

PREP	COOK
15 MIN.	30 MIN.

Jane Eyre is my favorite book, and I'm a sucker for any fog-shrouded British mystery. I can't get enough of the accents, the Queen's English, the tweed and wellies, the moody weather, and the fervent belief that a steaming cup of tea is a cure-all. Scotch eggs were invented at the London department store Fortnum & Mason and were packed in picnic baskets for members of Victorian high society on their way to Ascot races. These days, pre-packaged Scotch eggs are a staple at roadside service stations and are often eaten cold. Step it up a notch and serve these with a dollop of Olive Oil Mayo mixed with a little spicy mustard.

INGREDIENTS

- 2 pounds ground pork
- 2 teaspoons salt
- 1 teaspoon ground black pepper
- 1/2 teaspoon nutmeg
- pinch cinnamon
- pinch cloves
- 1 teaspoon dried tarragon leaves
- 1/4 cup fresh parsley leaves, minced (about 1 tablespoon)
- 1 tablespoon dried chives
- 2 cloves garlic, minced (about 2 teaspoons)
- 8 large eggs, hard-boiled and peeled
- 1 bag (2 ounces) fried pork rinds (optional)
- 2 large eggs, raw (optional)

DIRECTIONS

Preheat the oven to 375 F. Cover a baking sheet with parchment paper.

Place the ground pork in a large mixing bowl. Add salt, pepper, nutmeg, cinnamon, cloves, tarragon, parsley, chives, and garlic. Knead with your hands until well mixed.

Divide the pork mixture into 8 equal servings. Roll each piece into a ball, then flatten it in your palm into a pancake shape. Wrap the meat around a hard-boiled egg, rolling it between your palms until the egg is evenly covered. This is much easier than it sounds. If the meat sticks to your hands, moisten them with a little water. Place the meat wrapped eggs on the baking sheet.

If using the pork rinds, place them in the bowl of the food processor and process until they resemble bread crumbs; pour them onto a plate or in a shallow bowl. In another shallow bowl, beat the 2 raw eggs. Gently roll each meatball in pork rind crumbs; you want just a thin dusting. Then roll each meatball in the raw egg and roll a second time in the crushed pork rinds to evenly coat. Place on the baking sheet.

Bake for 25 minutes, then increase the temperature to 400 F and bake an additional 5-10 minutes, until the eggs are golden brown and crisp.

YOU KNOW HOW YOU COULD DO THAT?

Change the seasonings to take this very British snack around the world.
Eliminate all the seasonings in the original recipe and make these substitutions:

ITALIAN! *pork + 2 tablespoons Italian Sausage Seasoning or Pizza Seasoning (p. 49)*
ASIAN! *pork + 1 1/2 tablespoons Chinese five-spice powder + 2 tablespoons coconut aminos*
INDIAN! *lamb + 1 1/2 tablespoons curry powder*
MOROCCAN! *lamb + 1 1/2 tablespoons Ras el Hanout (p. 47)*
TEX-MEX! *beef + 1 tablespoon ground cumin + 1 tablespoon chili powder*

TASTES GREAT WITH

ROASTED SPAGHETTI SQUASH, P. 123
ZUCCHINI NOODLES AGLIO ET OLIO, P. 133
JICAMA "POTATO" SALAD, P. 137

Hard-boiled Eggs 101: Put eggs in a pan and cover with cold water. Bring to a boil, cover, turn off heat, and let eggs sit in the hot bath for 10 minutes. Drain the hot water and cover the eggs with ice water for 5 minutes. Drain and place in the fridge, until cold.

I'm not making any promises, but in Persian, rogan means oil and josh means heat, red, or passionate. Perhaps Rogan Josh is an aphrodisiac? I know it makes me feel good all over, and it's so scrumptious, it makes me want to marry myself.

ROGAN JOSH A TEXTURE LIKE CASHMERE FROM KASHMIR

SERVES 6 to 8

PREP
30 MIN.

COOK
1-2 HRS.

Rogan Josh is a curry dish from Kashmir, a region tucked among the borders of India, Pakistan, and China, all of which can be tasted in its fragrant blend of spices. I'd never eaten Rogan Josh before I bought the seasoning based solely on its enticing aroma, and now I'm not sure how I lived without it. Different cooks embellish their spice blends in different ways; this recipe is the one I devised in my kitchen in Austin, Texas. The resulting curry is rich and creamy with plenty of depth, but not too much heat.

INGREDIENTS

ROGAN JOSH SPICE BLEND:

2 tablespoons sweet paprika

1/2 tablespoon ground cayenne pepper

4 teaspoons ground cumin

4 teaspoons ground coriander

2 teaspoons chili powder

2 teaspoons ground cinnamon

2 teaspoons salt

3/4 teaspoon powdered ginger

1/2 teaspoon ground cardamom

1/2 teaspoon ground cloves

If you prefer, use 2-3 tablespoons of a commercial Rogan Josh spice blend. I recommend either Penzeys or Savory Spice Shop.

CURRY:

2 pounds lamb (stew meat, shoulder, or leg), cut into 1-inch cubes

salt and ground black pepper

1 tablespoon coconut oil

2 medium onions, diced (about 2 cups)

1 cup coconut milk

1 1/4 cups water

DIRECTIONS

In a small bowl, combine all the Rogan Josh spices and mix with a fork. In a large bowl, sprinkle the meat generously with salt and pepper, tossing with your hands to coat.

In a large pot or Dutch oven, heat the oil over medium-high heat, then add the lamb in batches and sear on all sides. Here's a tip from me to you: Respect the contact. Put the meat in there and let it be for at least 5 minutes, so it gets a nice brown crust – resist the temptation to stir it. Give it some private time, and it will reward you for your generosity. (Do that with people and get the same result. Neat!)

When the meat is brown, add the chopped onions and cook until the onions begin to soften and show brown spots.

Add all of the Rogan Josh spice blend to the pan and stir until fragrant, about 30 seconds. The spices really come to life in the fat, so let them revel in it.

Pour the coconut milk and water into the pot. Mix well, turn the heat to high, and bring to a boil. Cover and reduce heat to a simmer, allowing the meat to braise in the coconut milk for 1-2 hours.

When time's up, remove the lid and let the sauce thicken a bit, about 2-3 minutes.

YOU KNOW HOW YOU COULD DO THAT?

• *Use beef instead of lamb.*
• *Add sliced almonds to the sauce for rich indulgence.*
• *Sprinkle the top with Caramelized Coconut Chips (p. 153).*

TASTES
GREAT WITH

MINT CHUTNEY, P. 53
MASHED CAULIFLOWER, P. 113
CAULIFLOWER RICE PILAF, P. 121
ROASTED SPAGHETTI SQUASH, P. 123

I use pancake rings to make 3-inch egg foo yong patties. You can also make large, skillet-sized omelets instead.

EGG FOO YONG THE ALL-AMERICAN CHINESE TREAT

SERVES 2

PREP
05 MIN.

COOK
20 MIN.

Egg Foo Yong has a deliciously confused identity. It's not quite an omelet, almost a pancake, and somewhere beyond a fritter. It has become a 100% American dish, although its culinary roots reach back to Shanghai, and its name – with at least six accepted spellings – is Cantonese. Egg foo yong appeared in the first Chinese cookbook for American cooks in 1912, but reached the pinnacle of its popularity after World War II. The country was wild for Tiki culture and egg foo yong became ubiquitous in "Polynesian" and Chinese restaurants across the U.S. I was introduced to egg foo yong on a date with a very cute boy in high school; I was smitten with both.

INGREDIENTS

EGG FOO YONG:

4 large eggs

4 ounces grilled chicken thighs (p. 29), diced

2 cups steam-sautéed cabbage (p. 33), minced

4 scallions, green and white parts, thinly sliced

2 teaspoon coconut aminos

1 teaspoon Chinese five-spice powder

1/4 teaspoon cayenne pepper

1 teaspoon sesame oil

2 teaspoons coconut oil

additional scallion tops, for garnish

SPICY SECRET SAUCE:

2 tablespoons Olive Oil Mayo (p. 43)

1 teaspoon coconut aminos

1/2 teaspoon sesame oil

1/4 teaspoon rice vinegar

1/2 clove garlic, minced (about 1/2 teaspoon)

1/4 teaspoon crushed red pepper flakes

pinch cayenne pepper

If you'd visited the restaurant New Joy Young in Knoxville, Tennessee in the 1950s, you could have enjoyed a $3.20 feast of wonton soup, egg foo yong, chow mein, and egg rolls.

DIRECTIONS

Preheat the oven to 300 F. Cover a large baking sheet with parchment paper or aluminum foil.

In a large bowl, beat the eggs with a whisk or fork, then add the diced chicken, cabbage, scallions, coconut aminos, five-spice powder, cayenne, and sesame oil. Blend well.

Heat a large skillet over medium-high heat, about 3 minutes. Add coconut oil and allow it to melt. Place pancake rings in the skillet, and pour 1/4 cup batter into each ring. Cook 5 minutes, remove the rings, and flip the patties to brown the other side. Cook about 5 minutes, then remove to the baking sheet and place in the oven to keep them hot while you make the rest of the patties.

To make the Spicy Secret Sauce, place all the ingredients in a small bowl and use a fork to mix until blended.

To serve egg foo yong, stack the patties on a plate top with a dollop of Spicy Secret Sauce, and sprinkle with sliced scallion tops.

YOU KNOW HOW YOU COULD DO THAT?

Replace the grilled chicken with Char Siu (p. 91), steamed shrimp or crabmeat, grilled pork chop, or browned ground pork (p. 31).

TASTES GREAT WITH

VEGGIES WITH BEST STIR-FRY SAUCE EVER, P. 51
SESAME-GARLIC NORI CHIPS, P. 129
JICAMA HOME FRIES, P. 131

I considered several names for these meatballs, including Caraway'd Away Meatballs, Czechit Meatballs, *and (ahem)* Czech Out My Balls.

CZECH MEATBALLS INSPIRED BY MY PRAGUE ADVENTURES

SERVES 6 to 8

MAKES	PREP	COOK
about 36 meatballs	15 MIN.	25 MIN.

My maternal granny, Veronica Caroline Rovnak, came to the United States in 1902 from what was then called Czechoslovakia. Her village, not much more than a single street dominated by a white clapboard church, sat deep in a leafy green valley. At 17, she married my Italian grandfather in Pennsylvania, and they passed their fiery emotions to my mom and to me. I never learned much of Granny's personal history, but I liked to make up stories about gypsies and the evil eye. As a teenager, I gave myself chills by thinking of spies behind the Iron Curtain of Eastern Europe. When I finally visited Prague in 2010, it exceeded my romantic imagination. Everywhere I looked there was a story: in the cobblestone streets; in the statues atop the buildings; in the stained glass windows; and in the pubs where Czechs drink beer, eat hearty food, and swap tall tales about their everyday lives.

INGREDIENTS

- 1 clove garlic, minced (about 1 teaspoon)
- 1/2 tablespoon salt
- 1 tablespoon caraway seeds
- 1 teaspoon ground paprika
- 1 tablespoon ground black pepper
- 1 cup fresh parsley leaves, minced (about 1/4 cup)
- 1 tablespoon grainy mustard
- 1 large egg
- 2 pounds ground pork

YOU KNOW HOW YOU COULD DO THAT?

Make 'em tiny and serve on toothpicks as appetizers; reduce baking time to 10-15 minutes.

TASTY IDEAS

A SIDE DISH OF OLIVE OIL MAYO (P. 43) MIXED WITH A LITTLE GRAINY MUSTARD FOR DIPPING WOULD BE A FINE IDEA.

PILE THE MEATBALLS ON A BED OF SHREDDED RED OR GREEN (OR BOTH!) CABBAGE SAUTÉED WITH SALT, PEPPER, AND GARLIC.

SERVE ON TOP OF MASHED CAULIFLOWER (P. 113).

DIRECTIONS

Preheat the oven to 400 F. Cover a large baking sheet with parchment paper or aluminum foil.

In a large bowl, mix the garlic, salt, caraway seeds, paprika, pepper, parsley, mustard, and egg with a fork until combined. With your hands, crumble the pork into the bowl and knead until all of the ingredients are incorporated.

Moisten your hands with water and shake to remove excess. Measure a level tablespoon of pork and roll into a ball between your palms. Line up the meatballs like little soldiers on the prepared baking sheet, about 1/2 inch apart.

Slide the meatballs into the oven and bake for 20-25 minutes, until golden brown and cooked through.

NOTES

The Czech language is intimidating, which only inspires me to try to learn it. It uses 10 vowels but some words have no vowels, like vlk (wolf). So far, I've only mastered "cheers," so... Na zdraví!

This recipe is a paleo-friendly adaptation of a recipe from Cook's Illustrated, my favorite go-to source for technique that consistently produces excellent meals.

SERVES 8 to 12

PREP	MARINATE	COOK
10 MIN.	30 MIN.	1 HR. + 40 MIN.

I love nouns that are also verbs, words like cheer, smile, mug, and potentially my favorite – fork. In Cantonese, char siu literally means "fork roast," in reference to the traditional cooking method for this tangy-sweet BBQ pork which involves piercing strips of pork with a fork and roasting until they're tender and caramelized. This Chinese restaurant classic is usually seasoned with sugary, no-no ingredients like hoisin sauce, honey, brown sugar, and soy sauce. My marinade uses substitutions with minimal sugar and plenty of flavor. This recipe is not difficult, but demands your attention near the end. You'll forgive its neediness with your first bite of its sticky-crisp glaze.

INGREDIENTS

4 pounds boneless pork shoulder

MARINADE:

1/2 cup coconut aminos

1 dried date

3 cloves garlic, roughly chopped (about 1 1/2 tablespoons)

1/4 cup unsweetened apple sauce

1 teaspoon rice vinegar

1 tablespoon sunflower seed butter or almond butter (no sugar added)

4 teaspoons sesame oil

1/4 teaspoon crushed red pepper flakes

1 1/2 teaspoons powdered ginger

1 teaspoon Chinese five-spice powder

1/4 teaspoon ground black pepper

BBQ GLAZE:

1/4 cup tomato paste

1/3 cup unsweetened apple sauce

1/2 tablespoon rice vinegar

YOU KNOW HOW YOU COULD DO THAT?

Use a broiler: Instead of increasing oven temp to 500 F, you can use a broiler. Broil for 7-9 minutes before brushing with sauce, then broil 3-5 minutes per side after glazing.

DIRECTIONS

Cut the pork into 8 strips: Cut the shoulder in half lengthwise, then lay each half on its cut side, and slice lengthwise into 4 equal-sized strips. Trim off excess or hard fat. Poke each of the strips 10-12 times with a fork, then place the strips in a large zipper storage bag.

Place all the ingredients for the marinade in the food processor and process until combined. Measure 1/2 cup of the marinade and set it aside to use in the BBQ glaze later. Pour the rest of the marinade over the pork in the zipper bag. Squeeze out the excess air, seal the bag, and place in the fridge for 30 minutes to 4 hours. Flip the bag every once in a while so all sides of the meat are coated in the marinade.

While the pork is marinating, make the BBQ glaze. In a small saucepan, combine the 1/2 cup reserved marinade, tomato paste, apple sauce, and rice vinegar. Cook over medium heat, stirring with a wooden spoon until the sauce begins to thicken, about 4-6 minutes. You should end up with about 1 cup of sauce.

When you're almost ready to remove the meat from the marinade, preheat the oven to 300 F. Cover a large rimmed baking sheet or pan with aluminum foil, then set a wire rack on the pan; pour 1/4 cup water into the pan.

Remove the pork from the marinade and place on the rack, then cover the entire pan with aluminum foil, crimping the edges to form a seal. Roast the pork for 20 minutes, then remove the foil and roast an additional 40-45 minutes— watch for the edges to begin to turn a lovely brown.

Increase the oven temperature to 500 F and roast for 8-12 minutes more, until it's evenly browned. Carefully remove the pork from the oven and brush the tops and sides of the pieces with half the sauce. You want complete coverage with a thin layer so the sauce forms a glaze in the oven. As my dad would say, "Put it on like you're taking it off."

Return the pork to the oven for 6-8 minutes, until the sauce is a deep shade of burgundy. Remove the pan from the oven and use tongs to flip the pork. Brush the other side with sauce and return to the oven for the final 6-8 minutes.

Remove the pork from the oven and let it rest for 10 minutes, then cut cross-wise into 1/2-inch slices.

SERVES 2

PREP	COOK
05 MIN.	10 MIN.

My days of ordering Chinese takeout are mostly behind me, but I used to love the experience. Negotiating picks from the menu. Saying "Pu Pu platter" out loud. Watching the clock for the food to arrive. The inevitable grease marks on the delivery bag. Unpacking those distinctive white cardboard boxes. But you know what ruined the fun? The takeout food hangover from the soy, the sugar, the rice, the flour, the MSG, and the regret. This version includes the chewy-crisp nuggets of pork; vibrant, fresh vegetables; a nice salty bite from the coconut aminos; and the fresh snap of scallions. The fun is back.

INGREDIENTS

1 large head fresh cauliflower

2 large eggs

2 teaspoons plus 2 tablespoons coconut aminos

coconut oil, for sautéing

1/2 medium onion, diced (about 1/2 cup)

1 cup steamed broccoli florets, cut into
1/2-inch pieces (p. 33)

6-8 ounces Char Siu, cut into
1/2-inch cubes (p. 91)

2-3 scallions, dark green tops only, thinly
sliced (about 1/4 cup)

salt and black pepper, to taste

2 teaspoons sesame oil (optional)

2 teaspoons sesame seeds, for garnish
(optional)

You can use just about any veggies, but it's important to get the proportions right. If you add too many supporting vegetables, the ratio of veggies to rice is thrown off. Use about 1 cup of supporting veggies to every 3 cups of cauliflower rice.

DIRECTIONS

Break the cauliflower into florets, removing the stems. Place the florets in the food processor bowl and pulse until the cauliflower looks like rice. This takes about 10-15 one-second pulses. You may need to do this in two batches to avoid overcrowding. You should end up with about 3 cups of cauliflower rice.

Place the grated cauliflower in a microwave-safe container and zap for 2 minutes. This step preps the cauliflower, so it's almost tender before the stir-frying process. If you skip this step, you run the risk of the cauliflower turning to mush. You don't want BBQ Pork Fried Mush. (At least I don't think you do.)

If you're using the sesame seeds, heat a large sauté pan or wok over medium-high heat. When the pan is hot, toss in the sesame seeds and stir constantly until they're lightly toasted, about 3-5 minutes. Keep an eye on them! They can quickly change from pale white to dark brown in a blink. When you're happy with the toastiness, remove them from the pan and save for later.

In a small bowl, use a fork to scramble the eggs with 2 teaspoons coconut aminos. Heat 1 teaspoon coconut oil over medium-high heat in the pan, then add the eggs and stir with a wooden spoon until cooked through. Remove them from the pan and save for later.

In the same pan, heat 1 teaspoon coconut oil over medium heat, then sauté the diced onion until it's tender and translucent, about 5 minutes. Things are going to start happening a little faster now.

Add 1 tablespoon coconut oil to the onions and increase heat to high for about 90 seconds. When the pan is good and hot, add the cauliflower, scrambled egg, broccoli, and Char Siu. Stir with purpose! Sprinkle 2 tablespoons of coconut aminos over the ingredients in the pan, and continue to stir with enthusiasm until it's heated through, about 3 minutes.

Divide the fried rice onto two plates, then sprinkle each with half the chopped scallions and, if you're into the flavor of sesame, about 1 teaspoon sesame oil and 1 teaspoon of the toasted sesame seeds. Dig in with the sure knowledge that you are consuming at least two servings of vegetables, plenty of protein, and zero mystery ingredients.

YOU KNOW HOW YOU COULD DO THAT?

- *Replace BBQ pork with steamed shrimp or grilled chicken (p. 29).*
- *Replace the broccoli with slivered snap peas or snow peas.*
- *Replace half the broccoli with shredded steam-sautéed cabbage (p. 33).*
- *Add a handful of shredded iceberg lettuce during the final stir-fry.*

You can eat this with your fingers, like an animal. It's delightful. You can also serve it – with utensils, if you must – alongside pineapple, chopped cilantro, and lime wedges.

CITRUS CARNITAS
COULD SUPERSEDE BACON AS YOUR FAVORITE USE OF PIG

SERVES 8 to 12

PREP	COOK	ALERT
05 MIN.	2-3 HRS.	15 MIN.

The cooking part of this recipe takes about two to three hours, but at the end of that waiting period, you will be rewarded with caramel-brown, salty-tart, crispy pork that practically falls apart when you look at it. Isn't that worth a few hours of bubbling atop the stove? And the seasonings! The cumin is rich and earthy, the cayenne adds just the right bite, and the citrus juice creates a deep, layered flavor while it slyly tenderizes the meat.

INGREDIENTS

3-4 pounds pork shoulder, boneless or bone-in

1 rounded (!) tablespoon ground cumin

1 tablespoon coarse (granulated) garlic powder

1/2 tablespoon salt

1 teaspoon ground coriander

1 teaspoon ground black pepper

1 teaspoon ground cayenne pepper

1/2 cup lime juice

1/2 cup lemon juice

water

NOTES
I experimented with orange and pineapple juices, too, but lime and lemon was the best-tasting combo.

DIRECTIONS

With a sharp knife, cut the pork shoulder into a few large chunks. You don't want them bite-sized; I make mine about 3-4 inches across. Place the pork pieces in a large zipper storage bag.

In a small bowl, combine the cumin, garlic powder, salt, coriander, black pepper, and cayenne; mix with a fork. Add the spice blend to the bag, zip it closed, and shake assertively until all the pieces are coated with the spices. Feel free to add hips to the shaking action.

Place the pork in a large, deep pot. Pour the lime and lemon juice into the bottom of the pot, then add water to just cover the meat.

Place the pot on high heat and bring the water to a rip-roaring boil. When it's rolling, reduce the heat to keep a steady, strong simmer with the pan uncovered. The liquid should bubble a fair amount, but should not be a vigorous boil. While it's cooking, it will look like uninspired soup. Do not be discouraged! As the water evaporates, the powerful acidic qualities of the citrus juice tenderizes the meat.

At about the 2-hour mark, check the pot. The water should be much lower and maybe even almost gone. Things are about to get interesting! Allow all the water to cook out of the pan and watch as the meat magically fries and caramelizes in the pork fat and fruit juice. It is a thing of beauty – but now you need to pay attention so the alluring exterior doesn't burn.

Carefully turn the hunks of meat – without shredding them – to brown all sides, then remove the hunks to a plate and let them rest for 5 minutes before eating.

TASTY IDEAS

PAD THAI, P. 63

EGG FOO YONG, P. 87

SHRED, WRAP IN BUTTER LETTUCE LEAVES, AND DRIZZLE WITH SUNSHINE SAUCE, P. 45

Meat topped with potatoes isn't only found in the U.K. Natives of Quebec enjoy pâté chinois; the French eat hachis Parmentier; in the Middle East, it's Siniyet Batata, and in the Dominican Republic, they add cheese and call it pastelón de papa.

SERVES 4 to 6

PREP	COOK
30 MIN.	30 MIN.

Shepherd's pie is a traditional British or Irish dish made of lamb under a blanket of potatoes, and it's a kissin' cousin to cottage pie, made with beef. Cottage pie has been around since 1791. Back then, villagers topped it with potato slices that mimicked the tiles on a rustic cottage roof. This paleo version replaces the potatoes with creamy mashed cauliflower and can easily be doubled and frozen. With its short cooking time, this is perfect for a weeknight when you want to crawl into something warm and toasty.

INGREDIENTS

- 1 batch Mashed Cauliflower (p. 113)
- 1 1/2 tablespoons coconut oil
- 1 medium onion, diced (about 1 cup)
- 2 carrots, peeled and finely diced (about 1 cup)
- 2 cloves garlic, minced (about 2 teaspoons)
- 2 pounds ground lamb
- salt and black pepper, to taste
- 1 tablespoon tomato paste
- 1 cup beef or chicken broth
- 1 teaspoon coconut aminos
- 1 teaspoon dried rosemary
- 1/2 teaspoon dried thyme leaves
- 3 egg whites
- paprika, for garnish

DIRECTIONS

Preheat the oven to 400 F.

Heat a large skillet over medium-high heat, about 3 minutes. Add coconut oil and allow it to melt. Add the onion and carrot, reduce heat to medium-low and cover; allow the vegetables to get soft but not brown, about 5 minutes.

Add the garlic to the pan and stir until fragrant, about 1 minute. With your hands, crumble the ground lamb into the pan and break up large chunks with a wooden spoon. Sauté until it's cooked through and brown, about 5-10 minutes. Taste, then season with salt and pepper.

Add the tomato paste, broth, coconut aminos, rosemary, and thyme to the pan. Stir to combine, then bring to a boil and simmer uncovered until most of the liquid has evaporated, about 10 minutes. Set the pan aside and let it cool for 10-15 minutes. Beat the raw egg whites until frothy and blend into the meat mixture.

To assemble the shepherd's pie, spread the meat mixture evenly in a 12X6-inch (2.2 quart) baking dish. With a rubber scraper and a light hand, spread the mashed cauliflower on top of the meat. Gently drag the tines of a fork in a zigzag pattern across the surface to create a texture – the peaks and valleys turn a lovely golden brown in the oven. Sprinkle the top lightly with paprika.

Place the pan on the middle rack of the oven and bake for 25-30 minutes, until the top begins to brown. Remove to a cooling rack for 5-10 minutes before serving.

YOU KNOW HOW YOU COULD DO THAT?

COTTAGE PIE! *Replace the ground lamb with ground beef.*

ITALIAN! *Use beef instead of lamb, increase the tomato paste to 2 tablespoons, omit the coconut aminos, and replace the thyme with 1 tablespoon Pizza Seasoning (p. 49).*

CURRY! *Omit rosemary and thyme; add 1 1/2 tablespoons curry powder.*

MORROCAN! *Omit rosemary and thyme; add 1 1/2 tablespoons Ras el Hanout (p. 47).*

TEX-MEX! *Omit rosemary and thyme; add 1 tablespoon each of ground cumin and chili powder.*

MIDDLE EASTERN! *Omit rosemary and thyme; add 1 tablespoon ground cumin.*

TASTES GREAT WITH

CUMIN-ROASTED CARROTS, P. 115

SERVES   6 to 8

MAKES	PREP	COOK
about 50 meatballs	10 MIN.	30 MIN.

These meatballs came to me in a dream. I woke up with tumbling thoughts about a lush combination of pineapple, succulent pork, and creamy-sweet coconut. I was haunted by images of tikis and luaus. The only way to clear my mind was to surrender to the kitchen gods. After three attempts, something still wasn't quite right. Later, while lost in photos of tropical beaches and coral reefs, I landed on the fiery name, and the rest of the recipe fell into place. These taste even better the second day, so if you can endure the wait, you will be rewarded.

INGREDIENTS

1 1/2 cups unsweetened shredded coconut

1/2 teaspoon plus 1/2 teaspoon salt

3/4 teaspoon plus 1 teaspoon ground cayenne pepper

1 can crushed pineapple, sugar-free, packed in
  its own juice

2 tablespoons coconut aminos

1 1/2 teaspoons dried ginger

3 cloves garlic, minced (about 1 tablespoon)

3-4 scallions, white and green, very thinly sliced (about 1/4 cup)

1/2 fresh jalapeño, seeds and ribs removed, finely minced
  (about 2 teaspoons)

2 large eggs, lightly beaten

2 pounds ground pork

NOTES

Sprinkle leftover pineapple with crushed macadamia nuts and a dollop of Coconut Whipped Cream (p. 149) for a sweet tropical treat.

DIRECTIONS

Preheat the oven to 375 F. Cover a large baking sheet with parchment paper or aluminum foil. Heat a large non-stick skillet over medium-high heat, then add the coconut. Toast, stirring often with a wooden spoon, until golden brown, about 3 minutes. Remove from the heat and sprinkle with 1/2 teaspoon salt and 3/4 teaspoon cayenne pepper. Set aside to cool.

Drain the can of pineapple in a sieve placed over a bowl to catch the juice. You're going to use the juice later, so save it! Press the pineapple pulp against the sieve with a wooden spoon to extract the excess moisture. Place 1 cup of the drained pineapple in a large mixing bowl. (Save any leftover pineapple for dessert later.)

To the pineapple, add 1/2 teaspoon salt, 1 teaspoon cayenne, coconut aminos, ginger, garlic, scallions, jalapeño, and eggs. Beat with a wooden spoon until combined. With your hands, crumble the pork into the bowl and knead until all of the ingredients are incorporated.

Arrange the bowls of pineapple juice, spiced coconut, and seasoned pork for easy access. Measure a level tablespoon of pork to make a meatball. Lightly douse it in the pineapple juice, then roll it in the coconut, pressing the coconut shreds into the meat by lightly rolling the ball between your palms. This is a rare case in which more isn't better – don't go too cuckoo with the coconut. Line up the meatballs on the prepared baking sheet, about 1/2 inch apart.

Slide the meatballs into the oven and bake for 25-30 minutes, until sizzling and golden brown.

TASTES GREAT WITH

SUNSHINE SAUCE, P. 45
CONFETTI RICE, P. 121

SERVES 6 to 8

PREP	COOK	REST
30 MIN.	30 MIN.	30 MIN.

It's said that good things come to those who wait, and this dish may test your patience. Constructed with layers of tender eggplant, spicy homemade sausage, and silky tomato sauce, this casserole tastes best eaten a few days after baking. But the delayed gratification is worthwhile. A bite of the top layer, so tender and airy, is followed by a pleasant kick of heat that's soon tempered by the creamy eggplant.

INGREDIENTS

- 3 1/2 pounds globe eggplants (about 2-3)
- 2 tablespoons coconut oil, melted
- 2 pounds ground pork
- 3 tablespoons Italian Sausage Seasoning (p. 49)
- 1 tablespoon coconut oil
- 2 cloves garlic, minced (about 2 teaspoons)
- 1 (28 ounce) can diced fire-roasted tomatoes (I like Muir Glen)
- 8 large basil leaves, slivered (about 2 tablespoons)
- 4 eggs
- salt and black pepper, to taste
- 2 teaspoons extra-virgin olive oil

DIRECTIONS

Preheat the oven to 400 F. Cover two baking sheets with parchment paper or aluminum foil and brush a 13X9-inch pan with some of the melted coconut oil.

Slice the eggplant into rounds about 1/2-inch thick and place on baking sheet. Brush the eggplant with the remaining melted coconut oil, and sprinkle with salt and pepper. Bake for 20 minutes then remove from the oven and allow to cool. Reduce the oven temperature to 350 F for the next stage of baking.

While the eggplant is roasting, crumble the ground pork into a large mixing bowl with your hands, then add the Italian Sausage Seasoning and knead until well blended.

Heat a large sauté pan over medium-high heat. Crumble the pork into the pan, then break up large chunks using a wooden spoon. Cook until the pork is nicely browned, about 7-10 minutes. Remove the meat to a bowl and return the pan to the stove.

Reduce the heat to medium, then add 1 tablespoon coconut oil and the garlic to the pan. Cook until the garlic is fragrant, about 30 seconds, then add the tomatoes and 1 tablespoon of the basil. Stir to combine, increase heat, and bring to a boil. Reduce heat to low and simmer uncovered until slightly thickened, about 10 minutes. Season with salt and pepper to taste. Remove from heat and cool to room temperature.

When the tomato sauce is cool, scramble the eggs in a small bowl, then blend them into the tomato sauce with a wooden spoon. Warning: This will not look like something you'll want to eat, but soldier on.

To assemble the strata, place a single layer of eggplant in the bottom of the greased 13X9-inch pan. Sprinkle half of the cooked meat on top of the eggplant, then top with 1 1/2 cups of the sauce. Create another layer of eggplant, top with the remainder of the meat and 1 cup of the sauce. Build your final layer with eggplant and spread the remaining sauce evenly over the top.

Place the pan in the center of the oven and bake for 30 minutes. Remove the pan from the oven and let it rest for at least 30 minutes before slicing or eating. Before serving, lightly brush the top of the strata with the olive oil, then sprinkle with the remaining basil.

YOU KNOW HOW YOU COULD DO THAT?

- *Try a combo of 1 pound pork and 1 pound beef.*
- *Leave the meat out all together and use as a side dish or to feed vegetarian friends.*

If you're waiting a few days to eat it (good for you!), skip the olive oil and basil step when the strata comes out of the oven. Instead, wrap the pan tightly in aluminum foil and place in the refrigerator. When you're ready to eat, keep the strata covered in foil and reheat in a 300F oven for 20-30 minutes, then follow the garnish instructions.

If you're wary of the flip, you can cut large fillets into individual servings to make them easier to manage, but where's the adventure in that?!

SERVES 6 to 8

PREP	MARINATE	COOK
05 MIN.	30 MIN.	6-7 MIN.

Summers in Austin, Texas, are hot, humid, and oh so long. One afternoon, deep in the triple-digit days, a frosty package arrived on my front porch: a box of 18-inch-long salmon fillets direct from my friend Cheryl in the forty-ninth state. She's courageous and spicy, the kind of friend that's always in your corner. So when I made this recipe the first time, I channeled those qualities, gathered my courage, stood over the grill with commitment, and flipped that giant salmon fillet whole. I encourage you to do the same.

INGREDIENTS

- 1 tablespoon coconut oil, melted
- 1 tablespoon fresh orange juice
- 1 1/2 teaspoons dried ginger
- 1 1/2 teaspoons ground cumin
- 1 1/2 teaspoons ground coriander
- 1/2 teaspoon paprika
- 1 1/2 teaspoons salt
- 1/4 teaspoon ground cayenne pepper
- 1 1/2 to 2 pounds salmon fillets

DIRECTIONS

Mix the oil, orange juice, ginger, cumin, coriander, paprika, salt, and cayenne together in a small bowl to form a paste the consistency of thick salad dressing. This will transform into a gorgeous crust during grilling.

Place the salmon in a glass dish, massage the marinade over the salmon, then cover and refrigerate 30 minutes.

Preheat a gas grill on high with the lid closed for about 10 minutes, then place the salmon skin-side down, close the lid, and wait 3 minutes. Check the salmon; the skin should be a little blackened and starting to separate from the pink flesh. Take a deep breath, gather your confidence, slide a grill-safe flipper under the fillet, and flip! Breathe a sigh of relief, close the lid, and wait another 3 minutes.

Remove from the grill and eat like a cave person. I like to include a little piece of the crispy skin with each serving.

YOU KNOW HOW YOU COULD DO THAT?

- *Replace orange juice with lemon or lime.*
- *Try the spice rub on shrimp or white fish like cod or tilapia.*

TASTES GREAT WITH

CUMIN-ROASTED CARROTS, P. 115
CAULIFLOWER RICE PILAF, P. 121
EL MINZAH ORANGE SALAD, P. 143
TURKISH CHOPPED SALAD, P. 141

NOTES

Make a no-fuss salad alongside the salmon with slices of fresh avocado and mango sprinkled with minced red onion and fresh minced cilantro.

Party food! Divide your batter into several bowls, give each a different seasoning, then bake in mini muffin tins. Reduce baking time to 10-15 minutes.

MEAT AND SPINACH MUFFINS BETTER THAN THE BAKERY

MAKES *12 muffins*

PREP	COOL	BAKE
15 MIN.	15 MIN.	40 MIN.

These muffins are a savory surprise. First, they come in a brightly-colored wrapper, just like cupcakes, only better. They also have a pleasantly dense texture that packs both meat and veggies into a fun, portable shape. Great hot or cold, you can enjoy them as a grab-and-go snack or a sit-down meal.

INGREDIENTS

- 3 16-ounce bags frozen chopped spinach, defrosted
- 1/2 tablespoon coconut oil
- 1/2 medium onion, diced (about 1/2 cup)
- 1 1/2 pounds ground beef
- 2 cloves garlic, minced (about 2 teaspoons)
- 1/2 teaspoon salt
- 1/4 teaspoon ground black pepper
- 1/2 teaspoon ground cayenne pepper
- 3 large eggs

DIRECTIONS

Preheat the oven to 375 F.

This is crucial step! Squeeze the excess water from the defrosted spinach. Here's my trick for removing excess water: Place all the spinach in a colander or wire sieve and press out the water with the bottom of a bowl that fits inside the colander, then squeeze individual handfuls of spinach to wring out the remaining water. You should have about 4 cups of spinach when you're finished with the squeezing process.

Heat a large skillet over medium-high heat, about 3 minutes. Add coconut oil and allow it to melt. Toss the onion in the pan and sauté, stirring with a wooden spoon, until it's crisp-tender and translucent, about 5 minutes.

Crumble the meat into the pan, breaking up lumps with the wooden spoon. Add the garlic, salt, black pepper, and cayenne pepper and cook until the meat is browned. Stir in the spinach until it's combined. Set aside to cool for about 15 minutes.

Scramble the eggs in a small bowl with a fork, and when the meat is cool, add them to the meat; blend well. The easiest way to combine everything is to mix with your hands. Dig in!

Place muffin papers in a 12-count muffin pan; they prevent sticking. Pack the batter into a 1/2-cup measurer, then transfer it to the muffin pan, using your hands to pack the spinach tightly into the muffin paper. It should be slightly mounded on top – the muffins puff a bit when they bake, then slightly deflate when cool. Bake for 40 minutes until the tops are lightly browned. Remove the muffins from the pan, cool, and store covered, in the refrigerator.

NOTES

Omit the meat to make an unexpected spinach side dish that looks (and tastes) great alongside roasted meat or grilled steak – like popovers with more nutritional punch.

YOU KNOW HOW YOU COULD DO THAT?

Take your muffins on a world tour. Follow the directions above and add the following seasonings.

ITALIAN! *ground beef + 1 tablespoon Pizza Seasoning (p. 49)*

TEX-MEX! *ground beef + 1-2 tablespoons chili powder + 1 tablespoon lime juice*

INDIAN! *ground lamb + 1 tablespoon curry powder + 2 tablespoons raisins*

MIDDLE EASTERN! *ground lamb + 1 tablespoon cumin + 1 teaspoon dried mint leaves*

MOROCCAN! *ground lamb + 1 tablespoon Ras El Hanout (p. 47)*

GREEK! *ground lamb + 1 teaspoon dried oregano leaves + 1 tablespoon lemon juice*

ITALIAN! *ground pork + 1 tablespoon Italian Sausage Seasoning (p. 49)*

ASIAN! *ground pork + 2 teaspoons Chinese five-spice powder + 1 tablespoon coconut aminos*

Food historians wage an ongoing battle about the origin of Country Captain Chicken, which seems appropriate. The name most likely refers to a British sea captain, who carried the exotic flavors of the East to Britain and the American South sometime in the 18th century.

SERVES 6 to 8

PREP	COOK
20 MIN.	45 MIN.

In 1971, wearing a groovy vest-and-pants outfit she sewed herself, my mom won first prize in the Pottsville Republican's *annual Share-Your-Recipe contest. In the photo of the award ceremony at the swanky Necho Allen Hotel, she is clearly the hippest looking lady in the crowd. And she bucked tradition with her Country Captain Chicken recipe, too, omitting tomatoes and accessorizing with a sprinkle of bacon and almonds.*

INGREDIENTS

- 3 strips of sugar-free, nitrate-free bacon (optional)
- 2 pounds boneless, skinless chicken thighs
- salt and black pepper, to taste
- 1/2 tablespoon coconut oil
- 4 medium onions, thinly sliced (about 4 cups)
- 3 large bell peppers (red and/or green), thinly sliced
- 3 cloves garlic, minced (about 1 tablespoon)
- 3 tablespoons raisins
- 1/2 cup chicken broth
- 2 tablespoons curry powder (I like Penzeys Maharajah)
- 3 scallions, green tops only, thinly sliced
- 3 tablespoons sliced almonds, toasted (optional)

NOTES
To toast almonds, cook over medium-high heat in a dry skillet until browned, about 2-3 minutes.

TASTES GREAT ON A BED OF

MASHED CAULIFLOWER, P. 113
CAULIFLOWER RICE PILAF, P. 121
ROASTED SPAGHETTI SQUASH, P. 123
ZUCCHINI NOODLES AGLIO ET OLIO, P. 133

DIRECTIONS

Preheat the oven to 350 F.

Cut the bacon crosswise into 1/4-inch wide pieces. Place the chopped bacon in a cold skillet, turn the heat to medium-high, and fry the bacon until it's crisp, about 3-4 minutes. Remove from the pan with a wooden spoon and drain on a paper towel.

Season the chicken generously with salt and pepper. Add the coconut oil to the bacon fat in the pan, and reheat the skillet, about 3 minutes. Add the chicken in a single layer, smooth side down. Don't crowd the pan and don't annoy the chicken! You want it to form a crisp, brown crust, so place it in the pan and leave it alone, about 4 minutes per side. You may need to cook it in batches or be daring (!) and get two pans going at once. As the chicken browns, remove it from the skillet and place it in a single layer in a 13x9-inch baking pan.

In the same pan, without draining any remaining fat, sauté the onions, peppers, garlic, and raisins until the vegetables just begin to soften, but are not cooked through. Spread them on top of the chicken and return the skillet to the stove.

Pour the chicken broth into the hot skillet and use a wooden spoon to scrape up any brown bits. Add the curry powder to the pan and stir until the sauce begins to thicken, about 2 minutes. Pour the sauce over the chicken and wrap the pan tightly with aluminum foil.

Bake 35 minutes, then remove the foil, increase the heat to 400 F, and bake an additional 5-10 minutes. Before serving, sprinkle with scallions, bacon, and almonds.

YOU KNOW HOW YOU COULD DO THAT?

- *Replace the thighs with boneless, skinless breasts; increase the coconut oil for browning to 2 tablespoons.*

- *Add diced mango or apple to the chicken along with the peppers and onions.*

- *Garnish with shredded, unsweetened coconut.*

VEGGIES
& SALADS

A simple meal of meat and vegetables becomes something special with these recipes for surprising side dishes and cool salads.

A small handful of raisins, dried cranberries, or some toasted nuts would be a fine addition to this dish for a special occasion. Or Tuesday dinner.

CREAMY SPICE MARKET KALE

SERVES 2 to 4

PREP	COOK
05 MIN.	10 MIN.

Leafy greens like kale, chard, beet tops, and collards are the definition of "good for us," but I've never been a fan of the standard "throw in a pot with bacon, stew for hours, and hope for the best" approach. There is surely an elderly (but still elegant) lady in the South — who wears pearls, smokes cigars, and pours a mean mint julep — that can slow-braise greens to perfection. But she doesn't live in my house. So I turned to coconut milk and Ras el Hanout. With all due respect to Southern tradition, this trumps the tried and true.

INGREDIENTS

1 large bunch kale (or other sturdy leafy greens)

2 teaspoons Ras el Hanout (p. 47)

2 cloves fresh garlic, crushed (about 2 teaspoons)

pinch salt

1 teaspoon coconut oil

1/2 cup coconut milk

DIRECTIONS

Wash the greens and remove the tough stems with the tip of a sharp knife. Roughly chop or tear the leaves. Unlike salad greens, you want to let a little water cling to tough braising greens. The water droplets turn to steam in the pan and tenderize the leaves.

Heat a large skillet over medium-high heat, then toss in about half the greens. Stir them with a wooden spoon until they begin to wilt, then add the rest of the greens. Stir, then cover with a lid.

In a small bowl, mix the Ras el Hanout, garlic, and salt with a fork.

When the leaves are dark green and beginning to wilt, remove the lid and let any remaining water evaporate. When the pan is mostly dry, push the leaves to the side and add the coconut oil. Let the oil heat, then pour the spices directly into the pool of oil to release their fragrance (and flavor), about 20 seconds.

Pour the coconut milk into the pan, stirring to combine the greens, seasonings, and milk. Sauté until the sauce begins to thicken and your nose is delighted by the aroma.

YOU KNOW HOW YOU COULD DO THAT?

Try this with cooked spaghetti squash, other greens, or vegetables like green beans, cabbage, or broccoli. Simply adjust the pre-steaming time to accommodate their sturdiness.

Want to keep it basic? Toss washed and sliced kale into a skillet over medium-high heat. Add 1-2 tablespoons water, bring to a boil, cover and simmer 'til the kale is tender. Remove the lid and let extra water evaporate. Turn off the heat, drizzle the leaves with olive oil, then stir in salt, black pepper, and a crushed garlic clove. Sprinkle a squeeze of fresh lemon juice.

TASTES GREAT WITH

THE BEST CHICKEN YOU WILL EVER EAT, P. 69
GINGER-LIME GRILLED SHRIMP, P. 75
SCOTCH EGGS, P. 83
SALMON A L'AFRIQUE DU NORD, P. 103

NOTES

Use a sharp knife to cut along the thick stems to remove only the soon-to-be-tender leaves. Pile the leaves in a stack, then slice into 1-inch strips for leaves that look pretty and cook evenly.

MASHED CAULIFLOWER
CLASSIC COMFORT FOOD, REINVENTED

SERVES 2 to 4

PREP	COOK
10 MIN.	05 MIN.

I grew up in diner country, where creamy mashed potatoes were a standard side dish that almost defined a balanced dinner. (Hello, meat and potatoes!) This cauliflower proves that starch is not a requirement for comfort. Snuggled under a hearty beef stew or savory meatballs, mashed cauliflower is worthy of blue plate special status.

INGREDIENTS

1 bag (16 ounces) frozen cauliflower florets

1 garlic clove, crushed (about 1 teaspoon)

1 1/2 tablespoons coconut oil

1/2 cup coconut milk

salt and black pepper, to taste

1 tablespoon plus 2 teaspoons dried chopped chives

DIRECTIONS

Cook the cauliflower according to the package directions until it's very soft, but not waterlogged. Drain the water from the cauliflower and place the florets in the food processor.

In a microwave-safe bowl or small saucepan, heat the garlic, coconut oil, coconut milk, salt, and pepper, about 1 minute.

Puree the cauliflower in the bowl of a food processor, scraping down the sides. Add the coconut milk to the processor, along with 1 tablespoon of chives. Process about 10 seconds. Taste and adjust seasonings. Sprinkle with remaining chives before serving.

TASTES GREAT WITH

CINNAMON BEEF STEW, P. 65
THE BEST CHICKEN YOU WILL EVER EAT, P. 69
SCOTCH EGGS, P. 83
CZECH MEATBALLS, P. 89

NOTES

This can be made with fresh cauliflower, but the lovely, creamy texture is reached so much faster and easier with frozen. The nutrition of frozen stands up to fresh, so give yourself a break and opt for the easy way.

CUMIN-ROASTED CARROTS

SERVES 2 to 4

PREP 05 MIN. | **COOK** 20 MIN.

"The Incident" in my elementary school cafeteria left me cooked-carrot averse. (Think mean lunch lady, waterlogged carrots from a can, tepid milk, and force feeding.) But my mom introduced me to the sweet goodness of roasted carrots and saved the day. These carrots are tender, not mushy, with lovely brown bits and a flirty whisper of cumin that's brightened with a ping of mint. Take that, lunch lady!

INGREDIENTS

- 1 pound fresh carrots (about 10)
- 1/2 tablespoon ground cumin
- 1/4 teaspoon ground cinnamon
- 1/4 teaspoon salt
- 1/4 teaspoon ground black pepper
- 1 1/2 tablespoons coconut oil
- 1/2 fresh lemon (optional)
- a few leaves of fresh parsley and mint, minced, for garnish (optional)

"These were so good, I had to stop myself from eating the entire batch in one sitting! Love, love, love them."
—BurdNurd, a blog reader

YOU KNOW HOW YOU COULD DO THAT?

- Try slicing the carrots into 1/4-inch thick coins; increase roasting time to 30 minutes.
- Swap parsnips for carrots, or roast a batch of both for a colorful combo.

TASTES GREAT WITH

CINNAMON BEEF STEW, P. 65
MOROCCAN MEATBALLS, P. 71
SALMON L'AFRIQUE DU NORD, P. 103

NOTES

Until the 15th century, carrots were only available in purple, yellow, and red varieties. Those rainbow hues are making a comeback, thanks to local farmers and heirloom seeds. Look for white, yellow, red, and purple, in addition to the standard orange.

DIRECTIONS

Preheat the oven to 400 F. Cover a large baking sheet with parchment paper.

Wash and peel the carrots, then cut them lengthwise into thin strips, about 1/4-inch wide. Toss them into a large bowl.

With a fork, mix the cumin, cinnamon, salt, and pepper in a small microwave-safe bowl. Add the coconut oil and microwave until melted, about 15-20 seconds.

Pour the seasoned coconut oil over the carrots and toss with two wooden spoons until the carrots are evenly coated. Sing a verse of your favorite song so you don't skimp on tossing time. Do a taste test and adjust the seasonings.

Spread the carrots in a single layer on the baking sheet and roast for 15-20 minutes, until tender and slightly browned. Remove from the oven and squeeze the fresh lemon juice over the top. Sprinkle with the chopped herbs.

GREEK BROCCOLI
FRESH, BRIGHT, AND PRETTY ON THE PLATE

SERVES 2 to 4

PREP	COOK
10 MIN.	15 MIN.

Banish boring broccoli! In the time it takes to microwave a bag of the frozen stuff, you can whip up this fresh side dish that brings the sun-dappled shores of the Aegean right into your kitchen. The tender broccoli and tangy-sweet tomatoes relax in a sauce that's lightly flavored with Greek herbs. Opa!

INGREDIENTS

1/2 cup water

1 pound fresh broccoli, broken into florets

2 tablespoons extra-virgin olive oil

1 medium onion, diced (about 1 cup)

3 cloves garlic, minced (about 1 tablespoon)

1 cup fresh grape or cherry tomatoes

1/2 cup fresh parsley leaves, minced (about 2 tablespoons)

1/2 teaspoon dried oregano leaves

2 tablespoons tomato paste

1/2 teaspoon paprika

salt and black pepper, to taste

DIRECTIONS

In a large sauté pan, bring the water to a boil over high heat. Add the broccoli, cover with a tight-fitting lid, and steam the broccoli until tender, about 4-5 minutes. Drain the broccoli in a colander and rinse with cold water to stop the cooking process.

Dry the pan and heat the olive oil over medium heat. Add the onion, garlic, tomatoes, parsley, oregano, tomato paste, and paprika. Sauté until the onions are translucent and the tomatoes begin to pop. Add the broccoli and stir well to combine. Simmer uncovered 5-7 minutes until heated through. Taste and adjust seasonings.

YOU KNOW HOW YOU COULD DO THAT?

Replace the broccoli with fresh green beans or cauliflower.

TASTES GREAT WITH
HOT PLATES, P. 35
MEATZA PIE, P. 77

NOTES
No cherry or grape tomatoes? Use two ripe tomatoes instead. Remove the seeds, cut into 1-inch dice, and follow the rest of the directions.

A combination of whole and chopped pecan halves is the ideal blend of "pretty to behold" and "scrumptious to eat."

VELVETY BUTTERNUT SQUASH

SERVES 4 to 6

PREP	ROAST	BAKE
05 MIN.	50 MIN.	30 MIN.

The word "casserole" is so unassuming, so suggestive of "stuff from cans," it hardly seems appropriate for this dish. It's almost a confection, made of pillows and clouds and whispers. It starts as a puree that, while not bad on its own, is still just squash. But lovingly stir in a touch of coconut milk, Ras el Hanout, and an egg, and what you remove from the oven a short time later is smooth, spicy-sweet, and so far beyond a casserole, it deserves a new name.

INGREDIENTS

2 1/2 pounds butternut squash

2 tablespoons water

1 head garlic

1 tablespoon coconut oil

2 tablespoons coconut milk

1/4 teaspoon salt

2 teaspoons Ras el Hanout (p. 47)

1 large egg

1/4 cup pecan halves, chopped (reserve a few whole for garnish)

DIRECTIONS

Preheat the oven to 350 F. Cover a baking sheet with parchment paper. Cut the squash in half lengthwise and remove the seeds. Place cut-side down on the baking sheet and sprinkle 2 tablespoons of water onto the paper around the squash.

Peel the loose, papery skin off the garlic, and wrap it in a piece of aluminum foil. Put the baking sheet of squash and the foil packet in the oven. Bake 40-50 minutes, until the squash is tender. Set both aside until they're cool enough to handle, about 20 minutes.

Increase the oven temperature to 400 F.

When the squash is cool, use a spoon to scoop the flesh into the bowl of a food processor. Separate the garlic cloves and squeeze the roasted pulp into the bowl with the squash. Process the mixture to a smooth puree, then add the coconut oil, coconut milk, salt, and Ras el Hanout. Taste and adjust seasonings.

Beat the egg in a small bowl. Scrape the puree into a large mixing bowl and stir in the beaten egg with a wooden spoon until combined.

Grease the inside of a 3-cup casserole dish or individual ramekins with a little coconut oil, then add the squash puree. Top with chopped pecans and bake in the 400 F oven for 25-30 minutes, until the edges are a little bubbly and the top is golden brown.

YOU KNOW HOW YOU COULD DO THAT?

Skip the baking step and instead, make it a soup. Stir the purée into hot chicken or vegetable broth until desired consistency, then swirl in a few tablespoons of coconut milk. Add shredded, cooked chicken to make it a meal, then sprinkle the top with chopped parsley and a squeeze of fresh lemon juice.

Replace the butternut squash with other winter squash varieties like acorn, delicata, kabocha, hubbard, turban, or pumpkin. Sweet potatoes or yams will work very nicely, too.

NOTES

If you're using individual ramekins, keep an eye on the clock. You may need to reduce the second baking time to 15-20 minutes.

Pine nuts are traditional for pilaf in my family, but walnuts, pistachios, almonds, and pecans are all solid choices, too. The dried fruit can also be replaced with dried cranberries, figs, or dates.

CAULIFLOWER RICE PILAF
THE SENSATION OF RICE BACK IN YOUR LIFE

SERVES 6

PREP	COOK
10 MIN.	10 MIN.

I was the official rice maker in my family, and I perfected a water-measuring technique that involved placing my thumb against the bottom of the pan, just like my Sitti ("grandmother" in Arabic) taught my mom. I took great pride in my fluffy rice, and it was with a heavy heart that I banished my favorite grain from my diet. Then I learned the cauliflower trick, and my pilaf was reborn.

INGREDIENTS

1 large head fresh cauliflower

1 tablespoon plus 1 tablespoon coconut oil

8 dried apricot halves, minced (about 2 tablespoons)

1 1/2 tablespoons raisins

2 tablespoons pine (pignola) nuts

1/2 medium onion, diced (about 1/2 cup)

1 clove garlic, minced (about 1 teaspoon)

1/2 teaspoon ground cumin

1/2 teaspoon ground cinnamon

salt and black pepper, to taste

Quick salad! Toss cooked basic cauliflower rice with sliced olives, chopped parsley, sliced scallions, diced cucumber and tomato, a garlic clove, and equal parts lemon juice and extra-virgin olive oil. Let it rest at room temperature for about 20 minutes, then dig in.

DIRECTIONS

Break the cauliflower into florets, removing the stems. Place the florets in the food processor bowl and pulse until the cauliflower looks like rice. This takes about 10-15 one-second pulses. You may need to do this in two batches to avoid overcrowding (which leads to mush).

Heat a large skillet over medium-high heat, about 3 minutes. Add 1 tablespoon of coconut oil and allow it to melt. Add the apricots, raisins, pine nuts, onion, and garlic. Stir with a wooden spoon to combine and cook until the onions are translucent and the nuts start to brown, about 5 minutes.

Push the onions to the side of the pan and add the remaining 1 tablespoon of coconut oil. Add the cumin and cinnamon to the oil, then stir everything together – oil, spices, onions, nuts, and fruit – so they all mingle in happy harmony. When you can smell the spices, about 30 seconds, toss in the riced cauliflower and sauté until the cauliflower is tender, about 5 minutes. Try a bite, then season with salt and pepper.

YOU KNOW HOW YOU COULD DO THAT?

Same directions, different ingredients.

Turn your favorite rice into a one-dish meal – add diced, grilled chicken (p. 29).

BASIC RICE
Eliminate the fruit, nuts, and spices for a basic rice that's an ideal bed for meats, curries, and stews.

CONFETTI RICE
1/2 medium onion, chopped (about 1/2 cup)
1 clove garlic, minced (about 1 teaspoon)
1/2 medium green pepper, diced (about 1/2 cup)
1/2 medium red pepper, diced (about 1/2 cup)
1 medium carrot, grated (about 1/2 cup)
salt and black pepper, to taste

CURRY RICE
1/2 medium onion, chopped (about 1/2 cup)
1 clove garlic, minced (about 1 teaspoon)
1 cup diced fresh pineapple
2 tablespoons sliced almonds
1 teaspoon ground curry powder
salt and black pepper, to taste

BBQ PORK FRIED RICE (P. 93)

TASTES GREAT WITH

CINNAMON BEEF STEW, P. 65
MOROCCAN MEATBALLS, P. 71
SALMON A L'AFRIQUE DU NORD, P. 103

SERVES 4 to 6

PREP 02 MIN.

COOK 35 MIN.

I call bull on anyone who says, "Spaghetti squash tastes just like spaghetti." It does not. But it is delicious and nutritious, has the right shape, and can be twirled on a fork, so I accepted this vegetable substitute for pasta with an open heart. I was, however, repeatedly disappointed in the texture. I tried the microwave. I tried roasting it whole. I tried halfway submerging it in water while it baked. All of those methods resulted in a mushy mess. But now I've got it! I included this "recipe" so you, too, can roast your spaghetti squash to an ideal al dente.

INGREDIENTS

- 1 large spaghetti squash
- 3 tablespoons water

DIRECTIONS

Preheat the oven to 375 F. Cover a large baking sheet with parchment paper.

Cut the squash in half lengthwise. The easiest way to do this is, surprisingly, with a **small** knife. Use a sharp paring knife to carefully create a shallow slit along the top of the squash, lengthwise. Now, using a **large** knife, place the blade in the slit and bang the squash carefully with some force on the cutting board. It should crack along the fault line created by the small knife. Scoop out the seeds and pulp with a large spoon.

Place squash cut side down on the baking sheet. Sprinkle the water onto the paper around the squash. Roast until the squash is tender, but not mushy, 30-40 minutes. Place the baking sheet on a cooling rack, and, using a hot mitt, turn the squash cut side up to cool.

When it's cool enough to handle, scrape the inside with a fork to shred the squash into gorgeous spaghetti strands.

YOU KNOW HOW YOU COULD DO THAT?

In a hurry? You can cook spaghetti squash in the microwave, but it will not retain its al dente texture. Place squash cut side up in a microwave-safe dish along with 1/4 cup water. Cover with plastic wrap and cook on high for 10-15 minutes, depending on size.

NOTES

TASTY WAYS TO SPICE UP SPAGHETTI SQUASH.
TOSS WITH MELTED COCONUT OIL AND...

- GARLIC + CUMIN + CINNAMON
- GARLIC + CUMIN + CHILI POWDER
- CHOPPED CHIVES
- GARLIC + GINGER + COCONUT AMINOS + CRUSHED RED PEPPER FLAKES

TASTY IDEAS

HOT PLATES, P. 35
PAD THAI, P. 63

For tips on how to remain injury free while cutting spaghetti squash, visit www.theclothesmakethegirl.com/wellfed

COCONUT-ALMOND GREEN BEANS

SERVES 4

PREP	COOK
10 MIN.	15 MIN.

This could become the only green bean recipe you need. During the braising process, the sliced almonds almost melt into a rich coconut milk sauce that renders the elements indistinguishable from each other. And that's when you know the ingredients have fulfilled their destiny. Trust me: Make a double batch.

INGREDIENTS

1 tablespoon coconut oil

2 tablespoons sliced almonds

1/2 medium onion, finely diced (about 1/2 cup)

3 cloves garlic, minced (about 1 tablespoon)

1 teaspoon ground cumin

1 teaspoon ground coriander

1 teaspoon paprika

1/2 teaspoon red chili pepper flakes

3/4 teaspoon salt

1 cup coconut milk

1 pound green beans, trimmed

1 teaspoon lime juice

1/2 cup fresh cilantro leaves, minced (2 tablespoons) (optional)

DIRECTIONS

Heat the oil in a large sauté pan over medium heat. Add the almonds and cook until lightly browned. Keep an eye on them; they brown quickly! Transfer almonds to a plate for later. Resist the temptation to eat them!

In the same pan, sauté the onion, garlic, cumin, coriander, paprika, chili pepper flakes, and salt. Cook until the onion is soft and beginning to get brown bits, about 4-5 minutes.

Add the coconut milk to the pan and mix well, then add the green beans. Make sure everything is blended, then bring the pan to a boil, reduce the heat to a simmer, and cook covered until the beans are tender. The cooking time is a judgment call. If you like them crisp, it's about 6 minutes. If you like them softer, let them braise for about 8 minutes.

When the beans have reached the desired tenderness, remove the lid and let the sauce cook down until it thickens a bit. Remove the pan from the heat and stir in the almonds, lime juice, and cilantro (if using).

YOU KNOW HOW YOU COULD DO THAT?

Replace green beans with leafy greens like kale, collards, or chard and increase cooking time to 10-12 minutes.

TASTES GREAT WITH

GRILLED CHICKEN THIGHS, P. 29
GINGER-LIME GRILLED SHRIMP, P. 75
CITRUS CARNITAS, P. 95

NOTES

Should you find yourself lucky enough to have leftovers, you could treat yourself well by tossing the beans with thin slices of cooked beef, pork, or chicken.

Cauliflower is white, unlike its green cousin broccoli, because its protective leaves block the sun, negating its ability to produce chlorophyll.

COCOA-TOASTED CAULIFLOWER
COCOA IS A REWARD FOR EATING YOUR VEGGIES

SERVES 2 to 4

PREP | COOK

10 MIN. | 30 MIN.

White, gnarled, and so... solid, cauliflower can be difficult to love when it's raw. But roasted, it yields and becomes tender, almost creamy inside. The nutty flavor belies its bland color and holds its own against sturdy spices. Toasted in the oven with cocoa and the warmth of paprika, it easily overcomes its good-for-you reputation. Just right for a cozy evening when comfort food beckons.

INGREDIENTS

- 1 head fresh cauliflower
- 1 teaspoon paprika
- 1 teaspoon unsweetened cocoa
- 1/4 teaspoon salt
- 1/4 teaspoon ground black pepper
- 1 clove garlic, minced (about 1 teaspoon)
- 2 tablespoons coconut oil

DIRECTIONS

Preheat the oven to 400 F. Cover a baking sheet with parchment paper or aluminum foil. With a sharp knife, remove the core of the cauliflower and break it into florets. Place the florets in a large mixing bowl.

In a small microwave-safe bowl, mix the paprika, cocoa, salt, pepper, and garlic with a fork. Add the coconut oil and microwave for 15-20 seconds until the coconut oil is melted and the spices are fragrant.

Drizzle the spiced coconut oil over the cauliflower in the bowl, then toss with two wooden spoons until well coated. This should take at least 2 minutes. Name a food for every letter of the alphabet to amuse yourself while you toss. Do a taste test and adjust the seasonings.

Spread the cauliflower in a single layer on the baking sheet and roast in the oven for about 25-30 minutes, until it's tender and starting to get nice brown spots.

TASTES GREAT WITH
CINNAMON BEEF STEW, P. 65
CHOCOLATE CHILI, P. 73

NOTES
Use best-quality cocoa for the richest, deepest flavor. I like Penzeys Natural Cocoa Powder.

SESAME-GARLIC NORI CHIPS

MAKES *42 chips*

PREP 10 MIN.

COOK 15 MIN.

Sometimes I want to chow down like a teenager: just lie in front of the television, tune into something entertainingly mindless, and snarf a snack. But my ever-present adult voice knows that no amount of saltiness will ever recreate that fleeting adolescent combination of zero responsibility and boundless possibility. But that doesn't mean I won't try. When you feel like crawling into a bag of potato chips, whip up a quick batch of these instead.

INGREDIENTS

12 nori sheets

water

1 tablespoon sesame oil

3 cloves garlic, minced (about 1 tablespoon)

pinch ground cayenne pepper

salt, to taste

1/2 tablespoon sesame seeds

YOU KNOW HOW YOU COULD DO THAT?

Same directions, different ingredients.

SOUTHWEST NORI CHIPS

12 nori sheets

water

1 tablespoon coconut oil, melted

1 clove garlic, minced (about 1 teaspoon)

1 teaspoon paprika

1 teaspoon chili powder

salt, to taste

TOASTED ONION NORI CHIPS

12 nori sheets

water

1 tablespoon coconut oil, melted

1/2 tablespoon onion salt (I like Savory Spice Shop's Ornate Onion Salt)

1 tablespoon dried chives

DIRECTIONS

Preheat the oven to 275 F. Cover two large baking sheets with parchment paper or aluminum foil.

Place 6 sheets of nori, shiny side up, on the baking sheets. With a pastry brush, lightly brush the shiny side of the nori with water, being sure to reach the edges, then carefully align another sheet of nori on top and press them together. Repeat with the remaining sheets until they're all buddied up.

Using kitchen shears or a sharp knife, cut the nori into 1-inch strips, then cut those strips in half crosswise. You should end up with about 42 chips. Arrange the chips in a single layer on the baking sheets.

In a small bowl, combine the sesame oil, garlic, and cayenne. Use the pastry brush to coat the top the chips, then sprinkle generously with salt. Use your fingers to sprinkle the sesame seeds across the tops of the chips.

Place on the middle rack of the oven and bake for 15-20 minutes. They will crisp and turn a deep, glossy green. Remove from the oven, taste and sprinkle with more salt if you like, and allow them to cool before eating for maximum crunch.

TASTES GREAT WITH

MAKI ROLLS, P. 81
CHAR SIU, P. 91
BBQ PORK FRIED RICE, P. 93

The nori sheet was invented in Asakusa, Edo (now Tokyo), during the 17th century when the Japanese method for making paper was applied to nori paste. Nori sheets can be found in most grocery stores in the Asian food section or in the deli near the sushi display.

SERVES 2

SOAK	PREP	COOK
12-24		
12-24 HRS.	05 MIN.	20 MIN.

Diner home fries don't discriminate. The brown, crisp outside and warm tender inside are equally comfortable alongside eggs for an early morning (or midnight) breakfast and next to a beef burger. Seasoned with plenty of salt and just a whisper of paprika, these home fries transform jicama, the "Mexican potato," into an all-American classic.

NOTE: *This recipe requires you to pre-soak the jicama for 12-24 hours, so you'll need to start the process the day before you want to eat.*

INGREDIENTS

JICAMA:

1 pounds jicama

1/2 teaspoon salt

HOME FRIES:

1 medium onion, finely diced (about 1 cup)

1/2 tablespoon plus 2 tablespoons coconut oil

1 teaspoon paprika

1/2 teaspoon chili powder

1/4 teaspoon salt

1/4 teaspoon ground black pepper

1/4 cup fresh parsley leaves, minced (about 1 tablespoon)

DIRECTIONS

JICAMA:

Cut the jicama into 1/2-inch dice. Whether or not to peel it is up to you; I usually peel half and leave the skin on half to better impersonate a potato. When you're done chopping, you should have about 3 cups of cubes. Place the jicama and salt in a slow cooker and add enough water to cover the jicama by about 2 inches. Cover and cook on high for 12-24 hours. The longer it simmers, the more tender it becomes.

When the jicama has finished its soak, drain, pat dry, and place in the refrigerator until you're ready to start frying.

HOME FRIES:

Heat a large skillet over medium-high heat, about 3 minutes. Add coconut oil and allow it to melt. Toss the onion in the pan and sauté, stirring frequently with a wooden spoon. Cook until nicely browned, about 8-10 minutes. Transfer the onion to a small bowl and return the pan to the heat.

Add 2 tablespoons coconut oil to the skillet and allow the pan to get hot, about 2 minutes. Add the jicama cubes, shaking the skillet to make an even, single layer. Cook the jicama without stirring until the cubes are golden brown on the bottom, about 5 minutes, then carefully flip the jicama with a large spatula and make another single layer. Repeat this process until the jicama is browned on most sides, about 15 minutes.

When the jicama is appropriately toasty in color, add the onions, paprika, chili powder, salt, and pepper to the pan. Stir to blend and heat through. Remove the home fries from the heat, stir in the parsley, and serve immediately.

YOU KNOW HOW YOU COULD DO THAT?

Make hash! Add 1 cup diced bell pepper along with the onion and stir in Garlic-Browned Ground Beef (p. 31) after the jicama has browned.

TASTES GREAT WITH

THE BEST CHICKEN YOU WILL EVER EAT, P. 69
MACHACADO CON HUEVOS, P. 79
SCOTCH EGGS, P. 83
EGG FOO YONG, P. 87

NOTES

This recipe works equally well with white potatoes. Just boil cubed potatoes in salted water until tender, about 8-10 minutes. Drain well and proceed with the recipe.

Zucca *is the Italian word for squash, and in* France, Ireland, *and the U.K.,* zucchini *is known as* courgette.

SERVES 2

PREP	SWEAT	COOK
05 MIN.	20 MIN.	03 MIN.

Oh! The comfort of a warm bowl of slippery noodles that can be slurped or twirled with a fork to make big, soft, round bites; it's the kind of food you make while wearing pajamas and losing yourself in an excellent book. That's what this recipe is. The zucchini barely registers as a vegetable, so complete is its transformation to noodle by the olive oil, garlic, and almond flour "bread crumbs." It's warm, tender, familiar, and comforting. A hug in a bowl.

INGREDIENTS

4 zucchini, sliced with a julienne peeler (about 4 cups)

1/2 teaspoon coconut oil

1 tablespoon almond flour or almond meal

2 tablespoons extra-virgin olive oil

2 cloves garlic, minced (about 2 teaspoons)

1/4 teaspoon crushed red pepper flakes

1/4 cup fresh parsley leaves, minced (about 1 tablespoon)

salt and black pepper, to taste

A combination of both yellow squash and green zucchini makes for a colorful dish that's special enough to serve to guests, too.

TASTES GREAT WITH

GRILLED CHICKEN THIGHS, P. 29
MOROCCAN MEATBALLS, P. 71
CZECH MEATBALLS, P. 89
BLUE RIBBON COUNTRY CAPTAIN CHICKEN, P. 107

NOTES
A julienne peeler or spiralizer turns squash into noodles in no time – just slide the peeler lengthwise along the washed veggie.

DIRECTIONS

Place the julienned zucchini in a colander or wire strainer and toss generously with salt until the strands are lightly coated. Allow the zucchini to sit for 20-30 minutes to remove excess water. Rinse with running water, drain well, and pat dry with paper towels. (You may be tempted to skip this step; I strongly advise against it. This step ensures tender, rather than watery, noodles.)

While the zucchini is sweating in the colander, heat a large skillet over medium-high heat, about 2 minutes. Add the coconut oil, and when it's melted, add the almond flour and a pinch of salt. Sauté, stirring often with a wooden spoon, until it's toasty brown, about 2 minutes. Remove crumbs from the pan and save for garnish.

Return the pan to the medium-high heat and add the prepared zucchini noodles. Sauté them in the dry pan until just tender, about 1-2 minutes. Push the noodles to the side of the pan, and reduce the heat to low. Add the olive oil, garlic, and crushed red pepper, stirring with the spoon until the garlic is fragrant, about 20 seconds. Push the zucchini noodles into the oil and stir gently until they're coated. Turn off the heat and mix the parsley, salt, and black pepper into the noodles.

Sprinkle the noodles with the almond flour crumbs before serving. Slurping and ridiculously big bites are heartily encouraged.

YOU KNOW HOW YOU COULD DO THAT?

Make it a complete meal: Toss in grilled shrimp or chicken, or add a few scrambled eggs during the last few minutes of cooking to gently coat the strands with soft-cooked egg. Delizioso!

Omit the almond flour bread crumbs, then toss with Basil and Walnut Pesto (p. 53), Sri Lankan Curry Sauce (p. 57), or Sunshine Sauce (p. 45).

I like Ornate Onion Salt from the Savory Spice Shop, but any onion salt that pleases you will do for the French Onion Cucumbers.

RONI'S CREAMY CUCUMBERS
INSPIRED BY MOM'S SUMMER PICNIC BASKETS

SERVES 4

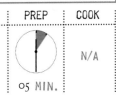

PREP 05 MIN. | COOK N/A

It was the 1970s, and most weekends, we pulled out the wicker picnic basket – fitted with nesting plastic plates, bowls, and cutlery in red, blue, yellow, and green – to go to the lake for swimming and grilling. My favorite summertime salad was Mom's cucumbers. The grassy-fresh parsley and piquant onions cut through the creaminess of the dressing and the almost-sweet cucumbers were cool and refreshing. To me, even in winter, this salad tastes like those lazy, carefree days.

INGREDIENTS

2 medium cucumbers, very thinly sliced into rounds

1/2 medium onion, very thinly sliced (about 1/2 cup)

2/3 cup fresh parsley leaves, minced (about 3 tablespoons)

1 teaspoon cider vinegar

1/4 cup Olive Oil Mayo (p. 43)

1 clove garlic, minced (about 1 teaspoon)

salt and black pepper, to taste

DIRECTIONS

Place the cucumbers, onion, and parsley in a large mixing bowl. Stir with a rubber scraper to combine.

In a small bowl, mix the vinegar, mayo, and garlic lightly with a fork until combined. Pour over cucumbers and gently fold until evenly coated. Season with salt and pepper.

TASTES GREAT WITH

GRILLED CHICKEN THIGHS, P. 29
GINGER-LIME GRILLED SHRIMP, P. 75
CITRUS CARNITAS, P. 95

If you're not in a hurry, you can make the salad even better. Toss the cucumber slices with a generous amount of salt and let them sit for 20-30 minutes in a colander to remove excess moisture. Rinse, drain, and pat dry with paper towels, then proceed.

YOU KNOW HOW YOU COULD DO THAT?

Same directions, different ingredients.

FRENCH ONION CUCUMBERS

2 medium cucumbers, very thinly sliced into rounds

1/2 medium onion, very thinly sliced (about 1/2 cup), sautéed in coconut oil until soft, then cooled

1/2 cup packed parsley leaves, minced (about 2 tablespoons)

1 teaspoon white wine vinegar

1/4 cup Olive Oil Mayo (p. 43)

1 clove garlic, minced (about 1 teaspoon)

1/4 teaspoon dried thyme leaves

1 tablespoon dried chives

1/2 teaspoon onion salt

black pepper, to taste

MIDDLE EASTERN CUCUMBERS

2 medium cucumbers, very thinly sliced into rounds

1/2 medium onion, very thinly sliced (about 1/2 cup)

1/3 cup fresh parsley leaves, minced (about 1 1/2 tablespoons)

1/3 cup fresh mint leaves, minced (about 1 1/2 tablespoons)

1 teaspoon lemon juice

1/4 cup Olive Oil Mayo (p. 43)

1 clove garlic, minced (about 1 teaspoon)

1/2 teaspoon za'atar (optional)

1/2 teaspoon crushed red pepper flakes or Aleppo pepper

1/2 teaspoon ground cumin

salt and black pepper, to taste

A FRESH TWIST ON A PICNIC CLASSIC

SERVES *4 to 6*

SOAK	PREP	COOK
12-24 HRS.	20 MIN.	N/A

Seemingly impenetrable, with an appearance between a potato and a rock, jicama is not the supermodel of the produce world. But remove that tough, dusty, brown skin, and you'll find a sweet, tender, juicy inside that's remarkably similar to a potato. Unlike potato, however, it can be eaten raw. Cut into slices or sticks, jicama is a refreshing addition to crudité plates. Cubed and slowly simmered, jicama softens and lives up to its alternative name: the Mexican potato.

NOTE: *This recipe requires you to pre-soak the jicama for 12-24 hours, so you'll need to start the process the day before you want to eat it.*

INGREDIENTS

JICAMA:

2 pounds jicama

1 teaspoon salt

SALAD:

4 strips sugar-free, nitrate-free bacon

4 large hard-boiled eggs, peeled and diced

1 medium stalk celery, diced (about 1/2 cup)

1/2 medium yellow or red onion, diced (about 1/2 cup)

1/2 cup fresh parsley leaves, minced (about 2 tablespoons)

1 tablespoon dried chives

3/4 teaspoon dried mustard

1/2 teaspoon paprika

1/2 teaspoon salt

1/2 teaspoon ground black pepper

3/4 cup Olive Oil Mayo (p. 43)

DIRECTIONS

JICAMA:

Cut the jicama into 1/2-inch dice. (Whether or not to peel it is up to you; I usually peel half and leave the skin on half to better impersonate a potato.) When you're done chopping, you should have about 6 cups of cubes. Place the jicama and salt in a slow cooker and add enough water to cover the jicama by about 2 inches. Cover and cook on high for 12-24 hours. The longer it simmers, the more tender it becomes.

When the jicama has finished its soak, drain, pat dry, and place in the refrigerator until you're ready to assemble the salad.

SALAD:

Cut the bacon crosswise into 1/4-inch wide pieces. Place the chopped bacon in a cold skillet, turn the heat to medium-high, and fry the bacon until it's crisp, about 3-4 minutes. Remove from the pan with a wooden spoon and drain on a paper towel.

Place bacon, eggs, celery, onion, parsley, chives, mustard, paprika, salt, and pepper in a large mixing bowl. Blend with a rubber scraper, then add jicama and mix again. Add mayo and gently fold until combined. Chill for 20-30 minutes before eating to allow the flavors to meld.

YOU KNOW HOW YOU COULD DO THAT?

Add 1/4 cup chopped dill pickles and/or 1/4 cup diced bell pepper.

NOTES

This recipe works equally well with white potatoes. Just boil cubed potatoes in salted water until tender, about 8-10 minutes. Drain well and proceed with the recipe.

TASTES GREAT WITH

BASIC GRILLED CHICKEN THIGHS, P. 29

SCOTCH EGGS, P. 83

CITRUS CARNITAS, P. 95

To toast sesame seeds, toss them in a dry pan over medium-high heat until lightly browned.

BABA GHANOUSH

SOMEWHERE DELICIOUSLY BETWEEN DIP AND SALAD

ABOUT *2½ cups*

PREP	COOK
10 MIN.	20 MIN.

Baba ghanoush is a Lebanese dish, but cooks in Egypt, Turkey, India, and even Romania have their own versions: a little more tahini here, onion instead of garlic there. Slightly smokey and laced with garlic and sesame, baba ghanoush is as much fun to eat as it is to say. "Baba" means father in Arabic, so I guess it's no accident that my dad taught me his way to make this timeless dish.

INGREDIENTS

2 pounds globe eggplant, about 2

1/4 cup tahini

1 teaspoon salt

3 tablespoons lemon juice

2 garlic cloves, roughly chopped

1/8 teaspoon chili powder

1/8 teaspoon ground cumin

OPTIONAL GARNISHES:

extra-virgin olive oil

a handful of fresh parsley leaves, minced

1 teaspoon toasted sesame seeds

Bonus! Tahini Dressing Recipe: Omit the eggplant and reduce garlic to one clove. Use the dressing as a dipping sauce for vegetables or drizzle it over cooked meat.

TASTES GREAT WITH

MIDDLE EASTERN TUNA SALAD, P. 67
THE BEST CHICKEN YOU WILL EVER EAT, P. 69

NOTES

DIRECTIONS

Preheat a gas grill or broiler on high heat with the lid closed, about 10 minutes.

Cut the eggplant in half lengthwise and use a sharp knife to cut a few diagonal score lines in the flesh. Place face down on the grill, close the lid, and grill for 5 minutes. Turn the eggplant face up, close the lid, and grill for an additional 10 minutes, until the skin is blackened and the eggplant is very tender (almost squishy). Set aside to cool.

While the eggplant cools, place the tahini, salt, lemon juice, garlic, chili powder, and cumin in the bowl of a food processor.

Scoop the roasted eggplant pulp out of the skin and place in a colander to drain extra moisture for 3-5 minutes. You should have about 2 cups of eggplant. Place it in the food processor and puree to your desired consistency.

To serve the traditional way, spread the baba ghanoush on a plate or in a shallow bowl and drizzle with olive oil, parsley, and sesame seeds. Use raw veggies and olives to scoop it into your mouth with abandon. Baba ghanoush tastes best at room temperature, but should be stored in the fridge. Its delicate flavor will hold up for 2-3 days.

YOU KNOW HOW YOU COULD DO THAT?

OVEN METHOD: *Place the oven rack in middle position and preheat oven to 500 F. Cover a large baking sheet with parchment paper. Poke the whole eggplant a few times with a fork and place on the baking sheet. Bake for 40-50 minutes, until the eggplant is very soft and beginning to collapse. Allow to cool, then follow the instructions above.*

A SECRET WEAPON FOR YOUR NEXT POTLUCK

SERVES 6 to 8

PREP	COOK
15 MIN. (all chopping!)	N/A

This is one of those recipes that makes everyone think you're a genius because it tastes so good (while inside you know the real secret: lots of chopping). Bright and crunchy, it's ridiculously healthy – without tasting like it's ridiculously healthy – and it's so friendly and eager to please. Cut the recipe in half if you don't want leftovers or double it up to share at a potluck.

INGREDIENTS

DRESSING:

1 cup fresh parsley leaves, minced (about 1/4 cup)

juice of 2 lemons (about 1/4 cup)

1 clove garlic, minced (about 1 teaspoon)

1/4 teaspoon ground cumin

1/4 teaspoon paprika

1/4 teaspoon dried oregano

1/4 teaspoon sumac (optional)

1/3 cup extra-virgin olive oil

salt and black pepper, to taste

SALAD:

2 medium cucumbers, peeled

2 medium green peppers, seeded

3 medium tomatoes

1/2 medium red onion

1 bunch radishes, tops removed

1 can (6 ounces) large black pitted olives

Make this recipe your own! Add other raw veggies like slivered red cabbage, fennel, or a few hot peppers. Toss in green olives instead of black, or roasted red peppers instead of raw. The only requirement? Chop everything into equal-sized dice, so no one taste dominates.

TASTES GREAT WITH

GRILLED CHICKEN THIGHS, P. 29
CITRUS CARNITAS, P. 95
SALMON A L'AFRIQUE DU NORD, P. 103

DIRECTIONS

Chop the parsley and place in a medium bowl. Add the lemon juice, garlic, cumin, paprika, oregano, and sumac. Whisk until blended, then slowly drizzle in the oil, stirring vigorously. Season with salt and pepper, taste, then adjust seasonings.

Dice all the vegetables into roughly the same size – a 1/4-inch dice is nice – and place in a large mixing bowl. Slice the olives and add to the bowl.

Pour the dressing over the salad and toss with two wooden spoons until the vegetables are coated. Taste and adjust seasonings.

YOU KNOW HOW YOU COULD DO THAT?

Same directions, different ingredients.

MAKE FRENCH-ISH DRESSING!
1 cup fresh parsley leaves, minced (about 1/4 cup)
juice of 2 lemons (about 1/4 cup)
1 clove garlic, minced (about 1 teaspoon)
1/2 tablespoon Dijon mustard
1 teaspoon dried thyme leaves
1/3 cup extra-virgin olive oil
salt and black pepper, to taste

MAKE ITALIAN-ISH DRESSING!
1 cup fresh parsley leaves, minced (about 1/4 cup)
4-5 fresh basil leaves, minced (about 2 tablespoons)
1/4 cup balsamic vinegar
1 clove garlic, minced (about 1 teaspoon)
1 teaspoon crushed red pepper flakes
1/3 cup extra-virgin olive oil
salt and black pepper, to taste

Rick's Café Américain, the location of skullduggery and heartbreak in the classic film Casablanca, was modeled after Hotel El Minzah.

SERVES 6 to 8

PREP	COOK
15 MIN.	N/A

The city of Tangier — perched on the northwestern tip of Morocco — was declared an International Zone after World War I and was jointly ruled by nine different countries, all reluctant to relinquish control of this glamorous port. The winding alleyways of the old city became a haven for smugglers, agents, double agents, and movie stars. Hotel El Minzah was the place to see and be seen. Like the motley cast of characters who sipped cocktails on the patio of the hotel, this salad brings together strong players —sweet oranges, cool fennel and mint, salty olives — that result in an enticing blend.

INGREDIENTS

4-5 large seedless oranges (about 3 pounds)

1 fennel bulb (about 1 pound)

1/4 medium red onion, very thinly sliced (about 1/4 cup)

1 cup large black olives, pitted and cut in half

1/4 cup fresh mint leaves, coarsely chopped (about 2 tablespoons)

2 tablespoons lemon juice

1 teaspoon paprika

1/4 teaspoon ground cayenne pepper

1/4 teaspoon ground coriander

1 clove garlic, minced (about 1 teaspoon)

salt and black pepper, to taste

3 tablespoons olive oil

fennel fronds, minced, for garnish (about 1/2 tablespoon)

YOU KNOW HOW YOU COULD DO THAT?

Add diced avocado for a creamy touch.

TASTES GREAT WITH

THE BEST CHICKEN YOU WILL EVER EAT, P. 69
GINGER-LIME GRILLED SHRIMP, P. 75
SALMON A L'AFRIQUE DU NORD, P. 103
CAULIFLOWER RICE PILAF, P. 121

DIRECTIONS

Use a sharp knife to peel the oranges, removing all of the bitter white pulp and the membrane on the outside of the orange sections. With your fingers, separate the sections and cut them into 1-inch pieces. Place in a large bowl.

Remove the fronds from the fennel and reserve a few for garnish. Cut the ends off the fennel bulb, and slice it very thinly, crosswise. Add the fennel, onion, olives, and mint to the oranges. Gently combine with a rubber scraper.

In a small bowl, whisk together lemon juice, paprika, cayenne, coriander, garlic, salt, and pepper. Add the oil in a slow drizzle, whisking continuously. Pour the dressing over the oranges and toss gently to blend. Let the flavors meld for about an hour before serving. Taste, adjust seasonings, then top with minced fennel fronds.

NOTES

"One of the wonderful things about Tangier was the fact that you could wear any mask you chose, provided you wore it with the proper dash and kept your story straight."
– from Two Tickets for Tangier by Van Wyck Mason

FRUITS

There is nothing wrong with a little something sweet from time to time.

You might be tempted to increase the amount of bacon and nuts. Who wouldn't be?! Most of the time, I'd agree with you. But the allure of this dessert is the subtle kiss of hickory and salt that makes the apples all the sweeter.

FRIED APPLES WITH BACON AND PECANS
AS EASY AS, WELL... YOU KNOW.

SERVES 4

PREP | COOK
10 MIN. | 05 MIN.

My one-stoplight hometown in Pennsylvania was tucked between coal mines and Amish country, so daytrips to Bucks County often ended in a diner where fried apples were almost always on the menu. This dessert strays from the standard Amish recipe, but I believe bacon is a worthy break from tradition. These tender slices of apple, dusted with cinnamon and sprinkled with pecans and bacon, melt on your tongue and taste like love.

INGREDIENTS

1 strip sugar-free, nitrate-free bacon

8 roasted, unsalted pecan halves, chopped (about 2 tablespoons)

1 tablespoon coconut oil

2 large, crisp apples, cored and sliced (about 2 cups)

1/4 teaspoon apple pie spice or cinnamon

zest from 1/4 lemon (about 1/4 teaspoon)

generous pinch salt

YOU KNOW HOW YOU COULD DO THAT?

• *Skip the bacon and nuts, then drizzle the apples with a spoonful of sunflower butter that's been warmed in the microwave.*

• *Use ripe pears as a stand-in for the apples.*

TASTY IDEAS

SERVE WITH A PORK CHOP, PORK LOIN, OR ROASTED TURKEY TO TURN THIS DESSERT INTO A SWEETLY SURPRISING SIDE.

DIRECTIONS

Cut the bacon crosswise into 1/4-inch wide pieces. Place the chopped bacon in a large, cold skillet, turn the heat to medium-high, and fry the bacon until it's crisp, about 3-4 minutes. Remove from pan with a wooden spoon and drain on a paper towel.

Wipe the grease out of the skillet, place it back on the heat, and add the chopped pecans. Stir with a wooden spoon until toasted, about 3-4 minutes. Remove from the pan.

In the same skillet, heat the coconut oil over medium-high. Add the apple slices and sauté until the apples begin to soften, about 2-3 minutes. In a small bowl, mix the apple pie spice, lemon zest, and salt with a fork, then add to the apples. Continue cooking until the apples are golden and fragrant, about 5 minutes.

Spoon into small dishes and sprinkle with bacon bits and chopped pecans.

NOTES

A mix of sweet and tart apples adds dimension, so consider Granny Smith with Pink Lady, or Braeburn with Honeycrisp. You can also go with Jonathan apples, the traditional Amish favorite.

Caramelized Coconut Chips are a salty-sweet surprise on top of a berry-delicious sundae.

GRAB A SPOON OF YOUR OWN

SERVES 4

PREP	COOK
15 MIN.	N/A

I've spent most of my adult life skipping dessert or requesting "just an extra spoon" from the waitress, so I could steal bites from someone else's plate. No more! It's such a lovely, tasty relief to eat paleo food and enjoy guilt-free desserts. The sweet surprise on the spoon with this dessert is the luxuriousness of whipped coconut milk. Chilled and flavored with a hint of almond, it's luscious and feels decadent. No sharing necessary.

NOTE: *This recipe requires you to chill a can of coconut milk in the fridge for at least 3-4 hours but, ideally, overnight.*

INGREDIENTS

- 1 can (14.5 ounces) coconut milk
- 2 cups fresh berries: strawberries, raspberries, and/or blueberries
- 1 teaspoon pure almond or vanilla extract
- 2 tablespoons sliced almonds
- 2 tablespoons Caramelized Coconut Chips (p. 153)

YOU KNOW HOW YOU COULD DO THAT?

GO TROPICAL! *With mango, banana, pineapple, and/or papaya.*
CELEBRATE SUMMER! *With peaches, nectarines, apricots, and/or cherries.*
MAKE IT SOPHISTICATED! *With grilled figs.*

NOTES

The Thai Kitchen brand of coconut milk separates very well when it's cold, and they make an organic version. That's always my first choice for whipped cream.

DIRECTIONS

This requires a bit of forethought: place a can of coconut milk in the refrigerator, ideally overnight, but 3-4 hours will do.

When you're ready to eat, put the can, a metal mixing bowl, and beaters from the mixer in the freezer for 15 minutes. While the coconut milk is chilling out in the freezer, gently wash the fruit and pat dry with paper towels.

Heat a nonstick skillet over medium-high heat. Add the sliced almonds and stir continuously with a wooden spoon until the almonds turn golden brown, about 3-5 minutes. Don't get distracted because they can change from toasty to tragic in a heartbeat.

When the coconut milk is cold, flip it upside down and open the bottom with a can opener. Pour off any liquid that's separated and scoop the thickened coconut milk into the chilled mixing bowl; add the almond extract. Whip on your mixer's highest setting until the milk is fluffy and has taken on the texture of whipped cream, about 5-7 minutes. Marvel at the creaminess!

Divide the berries among 4 bowls, then top with a dollop of whipped cream. Sprinkle each bowl with some of the toasted almonds and caramelized coconut chips.

Eat your dessert slowly with a spoon – then lick the bowl. Leftover whipped cream can be covered and stored in the refrigerator for about 3 days.

PEACH ALMOND CRISP
NUTTY, CRUMBLY, STICKY-SWEET GOODNESS

SERVES 4 to 6

PREP	COOK
15 MIN.	40 MIN.

Warm, tender fruit nestled under a blanket of cinnamon-scented, crumbly topping is the very definition of summer dessert. In each bite of sun-kissed peaches, you can taste warm rains, and dirt, and languid afternoons. Happily, this recipe works equally well with frozen fruit, so even in the deep of winter, you can recreate golden days so tasty, you will need a spoon.

NOTE: *This recipe is not approved for eating during your Whole30 – but it's a great way to celebrate after!*

INGREDIENTS

1 pound peaches (2-3 medium), cut into 1/2-inch dice (about 4 cups)

1/2 teaspoon lemon zest

1/2 tablespoon lemon juice

1/3 cup almond flour

4 dried dates, pitted

1/4 teaspoon cinnamon

1/8 teaspoon nutmeg

1/8 teaspoon salt

1 tablespoon coconut oil, chilled until solid, then diced

1/4 cup sliced almonds

DIRECTIONS

Preheat oven to 350 F.

In a medium bowl, mix the peaches, lemon zest, and lemon juice with a wooden spoon. Allow to rest at room temperature while you prepare the topping.

Place almond flour, dates, cinnamon, nutmeg, and salt in food processor. Pulse until combined. Sprinkle the chilled coconut oil chunks over the flour. Pulse about 10 times, then process on high for 5-10 seconds, until there are no lumps. Pour the topping into a bowl and use a fork to mix in the sliced almonds.

For an 8-inch square pan: Pour the fruit into the pan, pressing it gently into place with the back of a wooden spoon. Sprinkle the almond topping over the fruit and lightly press it into the fruit with the back of the spoon.

For individual ramekins: Place 4 ramekins on a baking sheet covered with parchment paper. Spoon generous 1/2-cup servings into individual ramekins, pressing the fruit into the ramekin with your hands. Press about 2 tablespoons of topping onto each ramekin.

Cover the crisp lightly with foil and bake for 30 minutes. Remove foil and bake 5-10 more minutes, until browned.

YOU KNOW HOW YOU COULD DO THAT?

Other sweet fruit and nut combinations:

1/2 POUND PEACHES + 1 POUND PITTED CHERRIES
  + SLICED ALMONDS

1 POUND PEARS + SLICED ALMONDS OR CHOPPED WALNUTS

1 POUND APPLES + CHOPPED PECANS

2 PINTS RASPBERRIES/BLACKBERRIES/BLUEBERRIES +
  SLICED ALMONDS

2 MANGOES + CHOPPED MACADAMIAS

2 PINTS STRAWBERRIES + CHOPPED PECANS

To use frozen fruit, defrost it in the refrigerator, then drain the fruit before tossing with the lemon zest and juice.

NOTES

This is best enjoyed warm – but not too hot – with a few tablespoons of coconut milk drizzled over the top.

And now, a coconut chip haiku:
Salty sweet and crisp
Not popcorn but paleo
Hail coconut chips

βΣ *a fruit, a nut, or a seed? It's all three. Botanically speaking, it's a drupe, a fruit with a stony covering that encloses the seed (like a peach).*

CARAMELIZED COCONUT CHIPS

MAKES   1 cup

PREP	COOK
10 SEC.	03 MIN.

Thursday nights in the Joulwan household, circa the 1980s, were "popcorn night." In sixth grade, I wrote an ode to popcorn, such was my devotion to the salty snack. Even though it's not on the paleo-approved menu, I still think of popcorn as my favorite food. These cinnamon-caramelized coconut chips do not taste like popcorn, but they do approximate the experience: the saltiness and mild sweetness, the blend of white and brown bits, and that ever-so-satisfying crunch.

INGREDIENTS

- 1/4 teaspoon salt
- 1/4 teaspoon cinnamon
- 1 cup unsweetened coconut flakes

DIRECTIONS

Mix the salt and cinnamon with a fork in a small ramekin and save for later. (The fun part!)

Heat a non-stick skillet over medium-high heat, about 2 minutes. Add the coconut flakes and distribute evenly, so they form a single layer in the bottom of the pan. Stir frequently. They begin to crisp and turn brown pretty quickly. This step takes only about 3 minutes, so pay attention! When the flakes have reached an appealing level of toastiness, remove the pan from the heat.

Sprinkle the hot coconut flakes with the salty cinnamon and toss until evenly seasoned. Transfer to a plate and allow them to cool in a single layer for maximum crunch. Store at room temp in an airtight container – if they last that long.

YOU KNOW HOW YOU COULD DO THAT?

Replace the cinnamon with one of these spices for international flair:

INDIAN! *1/4 teaspoon curry powder*

MOROCCAN! *1/4 teaspoon Ras el Hanout*

GARLICKY! *1/4 teaspoon coarse (granulated) garlic powder*

SOUTHWEST! *1/4 teaspoon chili powder + 1/4 teaspoon paprika*

ASIAN! *1/4 teaspoon Chinese five-spice powder*

(Thanks for the tip, David "Chef" Wallach!)

TASTY IDEAS

Sprinkle the original flavor of coconut chips with abandon on other dishes:

HOT PLATES, P. 35
ROGAN JOSH, P. 85
CAULIFLOWER RICE PILAF, P. 121
COCONUT-ALMOND GREEN BEANS, P. 125
BERRIES AND WHIPPED COCONUT CREAM, P. 149

NOTES

Enjoy a warming treat: Heat a cup of beef or chicken broth, add a crushed clove of garlic, and float a handful of Caramelized Coconut Chips on the top. Instant hug in a mug!

RESOURCES

This is your directory to the best sources for cooking tools, quality ingredients, and information about living paleo.

I tend to like what I like, and once I've found something I love, I don't usually experiment too much. That's why this is not a lengthy, comprehensive list of all the paleo resources out there. Instead, it's my personal list of bests. I use all of these myself, and I think they're top notch.

THE CLOTHES MAKE THE GIRL

www.theclothesmakethegirl.com
I update my site at least once a day with daring tales of my workouts, kitchen adventures (and disasters), useful bits of information to help you find motivation and inspiration in all areas of your life, and sometimes really good pictures of my cat, Smudge.

SHOPPING

My Amazon Store
www.theclothesmakethegirl.com/store
I'm a big fan of Amazon, because they have so many of the things I love. This store is my curated collection of "Good Stuff You Can Buy From Amazon," including essential kitchen tools that I use every day, the paleo books I read, "take me away" fiction, and a few other things that caught my fancy.

SPICES

These are my trusted suppliers for the magical substances that turn ingredients into meals. All three companies are owned by real people, not giant corporations, and have offline stores as well as online sales.

Penzeys Spices
www.penzeys.com

Savory Spice Shop
www.savoryspiceshop.com

The Spice & Tea Exchange
www.spiceandtea.com

GRASS-FED / PASTURED MEAT

These sites offer delicious, nutrition-packed meat, a wide variety of other healthy products, and reasonable prices (with deals for ordering in larger quantities). They're all staffed by real people who seem to genuinely care about their products and customers.

Lava Lake Lamb
www.lavalakelamb.com

Rocky Mountain Organic Meats
www.rockymtncuts.com

Tendergrass Farms
www.grassfedbeef.org

U.S. Wellness Meats
www.grasslandbeef.com

You'll find everything you need to develop healthy, happy eating habits at the Whole9 site. But if and when you're ready to learn more about different approaches to paleo eating, sink your teeth into these sites.

Whole9 – change your life in 30 days
www.whole9life.com

Robb Wolf – author of *The Paleo Solution*
www.robbwolf.com

Mark Sisson – author of *The Primal Blueprint*
www.marksdailyapple.com

Chris Kresser – author of *Your Personal Paleo Code*
www.chriskresser.com

Loren Cordain – author of *The Paleo Diet*
www.thepaleodiet.com

Sarah Fragoso – author of *Everyday Paleo*
www.everydaypaleo.com

Paleo Digest – aggregates posts from a wide variety of paleo and primal blogs
http://www.paleodigest.com

Modern Paleo – a moderated collection of paleo blogs that cover science, lifestyle, and recipes
http://modernpaleo.com

GET A COPY OF THE EBOOK FOR $1

Thank you for buying this copy of *Well Fed*!

As a show of our appreciation – and because I know some cookbook lovers don't like to spatter their cookbooks with tomato sauce or sizzling coconut oil – we're offering you a copy of the eBook (PDF) version of *Well Fed* for just a $1.00... and then we're donating that dollar to Common Threads, a non-profit organization that teaches low-income children how to cook wholesome, real food with a free 10-week, hands-on cooking classes.

For full details about the charity and to snag your PDF, visit **http://www.theclothesmakethegirl.com/well-fed-for-a-good-cause**.

Just add the PDF to your shopping cart and enter the code **GOODCAUSE** during checkout. You'll get a copy of the book you can print out and spill on with abandon, and a deserving organization will receive funds to support their mission.

Don't dilly-dally! This offer expires December 31, 2012.

MELISSA JOULWAN
Well Fed Author

Surprisingly, Melissa Joulwan's favorite vegetable is cabbage. Her favorite spice is cumin. Her favorite book is *Jane Eyre*. Her favorite city is Prague, and her favorite band is Social Distortion. You might have known all of that already if you follow her blog, The Clothes Make The Girl.

The Clothes Make the Girl is an unusual title for a blog that's about her tales of triumph and failure in the gym, in the kitchen, in life. She admits to being a sucker for the perfect little black dress and stompy black boots and sparkly what-whats. She may have started the blog going one way and wound up in entirely another. She says that her desire to be fit and healthy is almost matched by her love of punk fashion and high glamour.

Well Fed is her second book. Her first is *Rollergirl: Totally True Tales from the Track*, a memoir of her experiences as one of the founders of the Texas Rollergirls, the original Flat Track Roller Derby league. She has appeared on the Today Show and Good Morning America – in her roller skates and fishnets.

These days, she's hung up her skates, and her workouts are just as likely to include yoga and meditation, as lifting heavy things and trying to stay ahead of the CrossFit stopwatch.

Her favorite *Well Fed* recipe is Bora Bora Fireballs because it came to her in a dream – but Olive Oil Mayo runs a close second because it's so "spoontastically good."

DAVID HUMPHREYS
Well Fed Photographer & Illustrator

David Humphreys has, at different times, been an editor, a programmer, a project manager, a people manager, an illustrator, a photographer, a musician, and a designer. And that was just during this *Well Fed* project.

Currently, Dave has 675 items on his Amazon wishlist, including books on creative writing, cartooning and visual storytelling, portrait photography, living abroad (particularly in Europe), music theory, poster design, religion, electronics, computer science, crime, and Keith Richards. He also reads fiction. Last novel read: *Galore* by Michael Crummey. (Which is fantastic; you should read it!)

He considers himself quite lucky to be living with celebrity chef and generally fantastic person, Melissa Joulwan, and the best cat in the round world, Smudge.

His favorite *Well Fed* recipe is the Chocolate Chili, which he swears he could eat every damn day.

ALISON FINNEY
Well Fed Copyeditor

Alison Finney is a writer, copyeditor, and content lover, who credits Essie's many childhood tales of Toby the horse with her love of storytelling. Her work has appeared in *Texas Monthly*, *Austin Culture Map*, *Texas Tour and Meeting Guide*, and other Texas publications.

She grew up in the Texas Panhandle, where there were shootouts in the street every day at high noon and all food was served "plain and dry," to her liking. But eventually, she made her way to Austin, and now calls the city home and asparagus a friend.

There's an unbreakable tie between her two favorite *Well Fed* recipes: Peach Almond Crisp and Blue Ribbon Country Captain Chicken.

KATHLEEN SHANNON
Well Fed Graphic Designer

Kathleen Shannon is an ad agency senior art director turned freelancer turned brand consultant. She's also a local-sustainable-square-foot-gardening foodie, with a lacy-layeredy-boyfriend-jean aesthetic and a style perspective that pervades everything from her clothes, to her home, to her food. She'll follow a whim from the foothills of Mount Everest to a reality show audition just to have a good story to tell. Her approach to capturing, shaping and sharing overlaps her profession, her life and her blog at www.jeremyandkathleen.blogspot.com.

Kathleen is currently building a business with her sister called Braid Creative & Consulting, where they share their expertise on branding and being creative professionals with the world.

Her favorite *Well Fed* recipe is the Best Stir-Fry Sauce Ever. She loves it so much, she would like to marry it.

NATHAN BLACK
Well Fed Team Photographer

Nathan Black is a photographer, stunt man, door guy, and drifter. Since 2006, he has been collecting photos of knuckle tattoos – and the tall tales behind them – at www.knuckletattoos.com. He recently began a portrait project awkwardly

titled iwanttotakebeautifulpicturesofyou.com. He lives in East Austin with his three cats and two house mates.

His favorite *Well Fed* recipe is Pad Thai.

STEFANIE DISTEFANO
Well Fed Potter & Mosaic Artist

Stefanie is a potter, mosaic artist, and, perhaps, the very best kind of witch. Everything she touches in her pink-infused studio, known as FlamingO Ranch (www.flamingoranch.com), shimmers, glitters, shines, and glows. Her mosaics transform the mundane to the magical, and her handcrafted pottery graces the pages of *Well Fed*, as well as hundreds of stylish tabletops around the world.

She was mentored by the greatest mosaic artist on the east coast – Isaiah Zagar – and like her mentor, she is absolutely committed to and immersed in her art. You can see Stef's made-with-love pottery in the photos on these pages: 65, 99, 113, 121, 139.

After fulfilling the challenging role of neighbor and taste tester, Stef has determined that her favorite *Well Fed* recipe is Carmelized Coconut Chips.

Most lamb in the U.S. comes from Australia. G'day, mate!